THE GOSPEL CODE

Novel Claims About
Jesus, Mary Magdalene
and Da Vinci

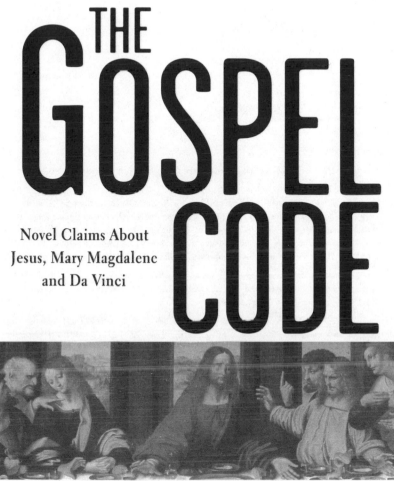

BEN WITHERINGTON III

InterVarsity Press
Downers Grove, Illinois

InterVarsity Press
P.O. Box 1400, Downers Grove, IL 60515-1426
World Wide Web: www.ivpress.com
E-mail: mail@ivpress.com

InterVarsity Press® *is the book-publishing division of InterVarsity Christian Fellowship/USA*®, *a student movement active on campus at hundreds of universities, colleges and schools of nursing in the United States of America, and a member movement of the International Fellowship of Evangelical Students. For information about local and regional activities, write Public Relations Dept., InterVarsity Christian Fellowship/USA, 6400 Schroeder Rd., P.O. Box 7895, Madison, WI 53707-7895, or visit the IVCF website at <www.intervarsity.org>.*

Scripture quotations, unless otherwise noted, are from the New Revised Standard Version of the Bible, copyright 1989 by the Division of Christian Education of the National Council of the Churches of Christ in the USA. Used by permission. All rights reserved.

"One of Us" by Eric Bazilian ©1995 *Human Boy Music (ASCAP). All rights on behalf of Human Boy Music (ASCAP). Administered by WB Music Corp. (ASCAP). All rights reserved. Used by permission of Warner Bros. Publications U.S. Inc., Miami, FL.*

Design: Cindy Kiple

Images: The Last Supper, *Reunion des Musees Nationaux/Art Resource, NY*

ISBN 0-8308-3267-X

Printed in the United States of America ∞

Library of Congress Cataloging-in-Publication Data

Witherington, Ben, 1951-
    The Gospel code: novel claims about Jesus, Mary Magdalene, and da
Vinci/Ben Witherington III.
        p. cm.
    Includes bibliographical references and index.
    ISBN 0-8308-3267-X (pbk.: alk. paper)
    1. Brown, Dan, 1964- Da Vinci code. 2. Mary Magdalene, Saint—In
literature. 3. Christian saints in literature. 4. Jesus Christ—In
literature. 5. Christianity in literature. I. Title.
PS3552.R685434D339 2004
813'.54—dc22   2004006655

| P | 19 | 18 | 17 | 16 | 15 | 14 | 13 | 12 | 11 | 10 | 9 | 8 | 7 | 6 | 5 | 4 | 3 | 2 |
| Y | 20 | 19 | 18 | 17 | 16 | 15 | 14 | 13 | 12 | 11 | 10 | 09 | 08 | 07 | 06 | 05 | 04 |

THE SECOND COMING

W. B. Yeats

Turning and turning in the widening gyre
The falcon cannot hear the falconer;
Things fall apart; the centre cannot hold;
Mere anarchy is loosed upon the world,
The blood-dimmed tide is loosed, and everywhere
The ceremony of innocence is drowned;
The best lack all conviction, while the worst
Are full of passionate intensity.
Surely some revelation is at hand;
Surely the Second Coming is at hand.
The Second Coming! Hardly are those words out
When a vast image out of *Spiritus Mundi*
Troubles my sight: somewhere in sands of the desert
A shape with lion body and the head of a man,
A gaze blank and pitiless as the sun,
Is moving its slow thighs, while all about it
Reel shadows of the indignant desert birds.
The darkness drops again; but now I know
That twenty centuries of stony sleep
Were vexed to nightmare by a rocking cradle,
And what rough beast, its hour come round at last,
Slouches toward Bethlehem to be born?

CONTENTS

Acknowledgments

I wish to thank Jim Hoover, a longtime friend, for suggesting this project to me. Without the editing help of Jim and Drew Blankman this book could never have been completed in good time and good order.

PREFACE

Western culture is a Jesus-haunted culture, and yet one that is largely biblically illiterate. Almost anything can pass for knowledge of Jesus and early Christianity in such a culture. I was doing a radio show last year when a lady called from her car. She was stuck in traffic on the Santa Monica freeway and was listening to the show. She said, "I am sitting here in traffic holding on to my crystals and feeling really close to Jesus, and I am wondering, what is the connection between these crystals and Jesus?" My instant and instinctive response was to say, "Nothing, except that he made those crystals."

Today, those who promise to reveal secrets about Jesus—secrets long suppressed by the church and other religious institutions, secrets that may be scandalous or at least that debunk traditional views of Jesus and early Christianity—have an instant audience. Throw in a conspiracy theory and take an anti-establishment approach, and the audience is hooked. In a culture where the latest is the greatest and the old is suspect, it is no wonder that *The Da Vinci Code* has been atop the *New York Times* bestseller list for over forty weeks. Even a serious religious book like Elaine Pagels's *Beyond Belief*, which offers up scholarly support for some things the novel suggests, has cracked the top 100.

While many traditional Christians might be tempted to scoff at and dismiss such books as either mere fiction or the opinions of a few fringe scholars, this would be a serious mistake. We are facing a serious revolution regarding some of the long-held truths about Jesus, early Christianity and the Bible.

It is no accident that in the 1990s we were regaled time and again by the revelations of the Jesus Seminar. This group of scholars dismembered Jesus' teachings and then divided them into genuine and inauthentic parts. It is no accident that we have well-known figures like Bishop Spong or Marcus Borg proclaiming a new Christianity for a new age. They are John the Baptists heralding the coming of the new syncretism of New Age religion—part pagan, part gnostic and part Christian. It is no accident that a mainline denomination has now ordained a gay bishop, and gay marriage is already being legalized in various places. It is no accident that a judge in the Bible Belt was censured for putting up a monument to the Ten Commandments in a public place, commandments that were part of the basis of every Western law code, including America's. Our culture is experiencing a sea change, and the old Judeo-Christian ways of thinking about things are being challenged at their very foundations.

Now novels such as *The Da Vinci Code* are disseminating this new syncretism to the masses. A follow-up movie, directed by Ron Howard and with a world-class cast, is soon to follow, while the wonderful *Gospel of John* movie is largely ignored by the general public and Mel Gibson's *The Passion of the Christ* is mired in controversy and objections. As I write this, I am being asked to go to one church after another to explain and decipher Dan Brown's novel. It appears that we are in an age where a New Testament prophecy has come true—"For the time is coming when people will not put up with sound doctrine, but having itching ears, they will accumulate for themselves teachers to suit their own desires, and will turn away from listening to the truth and wander away to myths" (2 Timothy 4:3-4). These seem to be such times, when people will indeed believe things that are "beyond belief." This book is intended as a wake-up call to those who have not been noticing the signs of the times.

To avoid cluttering the text with note numbers, I have identified my sources and given additional information in a set of notes at the back of this book. See page 185 for a further explanation of how to use them.

PART ONE

VENI, VIDI, DA VINCI

A NOVEL IDEA?

O n the surface of things, all seems well. You pick up a copy of Dan Brown's bestseller *The Da Vinci Code*. What could be more fun than reading a real page turner? This books captures your attention and holds it as well as any John Grisham novel.

Yet for those who have been reading sensational claims about early Christianity over the years, there is something strangely familiar about this book. Wasn't there a book very much like this one published some twenty years ago? Below is the editorial review from Amazon.com of *Holy Blood, Holy Grail*, which came out in 1982:

> Michael Baigent, Henry Lincoln, and Richard Leigh, authors of *The Messianic Legacy*, spent over 10 years on their own kind of quest for the Holy Grail, into the secretive history of early France. What they found, researched with the tenacity and attention to detail that befits any great quest, is a tangled and intricate story of politics and faith that reads like a mystery novel. It is the story of the Knights Templar, and a behind-the-scenes society called the Prieure de Sion, and its involvement in reinstating descendants of the Merovingian bloodline into political power. Why? The authors of *Holy Blood, Holy Grail* assert that their explorations into early history ultimately reveal that Jesus may not have died on the cross, but lived to marry and father children whose bloodline continues today. The authors' point here is not to compromise or to demean Jesus, but to offer another, more complete perspective of Jesus as God's incarnation in man. The

power of this secret, which has been carefully guarded for hundreds of years, has sparked much controversy. For all the sensationalism and hoopla surrounding *Holy Blood, Holy Grail* and the alternate history that it outlines, the authors are careful to keep their perspective and sense of skepticism alive in its pages, explaining carefully and clearly how they came to draw such combustible conclusions. — *Jodie Buller*

And the inside-flap copy asks:

- Is the traditional, accepted view of the life of Christ in some way incomplete?

- Is it possible Christ did not die on the cross?

- Is it possible Jesus was married, a father, and that his bloodline still exists?

- Is it possible that parchments found in the South of France a century ago reveal one of the best-kept secrets of Christendom?

- Is it possible that these parchments contain the very heart of the mystery of the Holy Grail?

Or consider the 1993 book written by a woman who says that reading *Holy Blood, Holy Grail* changed her life—Margaret Starbird's *The Woman with the Alabaster Jar: Mary Magdalen and the Holy Grail.* In this book Starbird is reacting to what she sees as the repression and exclusion of women in the Roman Catholic tradition. Unfortunately, what she offers us is a story of Mary Magdalene (who she wrongly identifies with Mary of Bethany, who anointed Jesus). According to Starbird, Mary Magdalene was Jesus' wife, and she became the Holy Grail in the sense of bearing Jesus' children and passing along the holy blood. Ultimately Starbird relies more on medieval lore and art, and she fails to take the Bible seriously.

There was a tendency in medieval exegesis, beginning with Gregory the Great, to identify Mary Magdalene with the sinful woman of Luke 7:36-50 and sometimes also with Mary of Bethany. We will deal with the former mistake shortly, but here it needs to be noted that a woman who is identified as from Magdala (Mary Magdalene) cannot be identified at the same time and in the same Gospel as from Bethany (see John 12:1-3 and John 19:25). Geographical designations were used in a fixed way to say where a person was from, not where they might be currently living. This was done because it was believed that a person's origin said something definitive about (and sometimes even determined) who that person was or could be, hence Nathaniel's question about whether anything good could come out of Nazareth (John 1:46). In that culture, geography, gender and generation (parentage) were thought to determine identity and personality.

In a culture where there were no last names, a geographical designation was one of the main ways to distinguish people with the same first name, and it appears the geographical designation was regularly used of *those who never married*, especially women who could not use the patronymic ("son of . . .": as in Simon bar-Jonah, which means "Simon, the son of John"). In the Greek New Testament, for example, in Luke 8:1-3 Joanna is identified by the phrase "of Chuza," which surely means "wife of Chuza," but in the same list Mary is said to be "of Magdala." Had Mary of Magdala been married to Jesus, she would have been identified in the same way as Joanna, not with the geographical designation.

Once *Holy Blood, Holy Grail* and *The Woman with the Alabaster Jar* are examined and we turn to *The Da Vinci Code*, we realize we've been down this road before—*twice!* Only now it's being served up in a novel that purports to be based on the facts unearthed by Baigent, Lincoln, Leigh, Starbird and others. Lest we think that Dan Brown intends for his book to be seen as pure fiction, we are told on the very first page of his work titled *FACT* that not only is there a Priory of Sion and a Catholic sect known as Opus Dei, but "all descriptions of artwork, architecture, documents, and secret rituals in this novel are accurate."

Our concern isn't so much with Brown's ability to describe art or architecture accurately (though we will question his interpretation of da Vinci's famous painting of the Last Supper), but rather with his handling of ancient documents and his treatment of early Christian history. In these realms he is not merely out of his depth, he is also a purveyor of errors of both fact and interpretation, including some mistakes that even the most amateur student of religious history should never make.

He can't hide behind the disclaimer that "this is fiction" because his very first page intends to give the impression that it is a novel grounded solidly in history. He presents his work as historical fiction: though the main characters and their drama are fictional, the materials they are seeking and studying are portrayed as facts or at least probably true. There should have been a caveat emptor—"let the buyer beware"—on page one.

When you read a compelling work of fiction and incongruities keep popping up, here a detail doesn't ring true or there a fact seems to be in error, the apparent authenticity of the work is ruined. Brown didn't have much to worry about since his readers are largely unattuned to religious and historical errors. Indeed, many of them apparently take at face value what the main characters in this work—Robert Langdon, the famous professor of religious symbols from Harvard, and Leigh Teabing, the historical expert and longtime quester after the Grail—say about Jesus and the history of early Christianity. It really doesn't matter that because of his greed for the Grail, Teabing turns out to be a rogue and a scoundrel. Neither Langdon nor anyone else repudiates Teabing's historical claims at the end of the novel. Indeed, the novel concludes at the Louvre with "proof" that what the book claims about Mary Magdalene is really true. After all, page one says, "all descriptions of artwork, architecture, documents, and secret rituals in this novel are accurate." But is there really an artistic shrine or tomb of Mary Magdalene in the Louvre?

There is another factor at play in what appears to be fiction, another central character whose name, not coincidentally, is Sophie Neveu, and who, also not coincidentally, is an expert in cracking codes. Her name gives her identity away to anyone who knows Greek or early Jewish and Christian literature. Her name means "New Wisdom," and as the novel progresses she receives enlightenment through the revelations unfolded by Teabing and

Langdon. Sophie is a symbol for Brown's audience of neophytes, eager to learn the secrets, crack the codes and have their collective religious consciousness raised. She represents the postmodern American public—who is in for the education of a lifetime. In the process she learns her own history and past, and how it fits into the Grail story itself. At the end of the novel we learn that Sophie is a descendent of Jesus and Mary Magdalene, the Holy Grail! The answer to the religious quest lies within herself, within her own bloodline.

Sophie Neveu represents the modern public seeking insider knowledge (*gnosis*) so she can understand the secret of her own identity. And not surprisingly, the quest leads ultimately within rather than outside the seeker. This is a very different vision of salvation than the apostle Paul's, who says, "if anyone is in Christ, there is a new creation" (2 Corinthians 5:17). In Brown's novel, salvation is a matter of getting to the bottom of our self to understand our own identity. In other words, the religious quest ultimately leads us back to our own self, an exercise in pure narcissism! The notion of Jesus' being the Savior is repudiated. In the book he is just a great teacher and perhaps a prophet.

But this new insider knowledge, this new wisdom that Sophie embodies in name and nature, has a further dimension: the "sacred feminine." Here Brown revives the old pagan fertility cult and goddess worship. Sophie Neveu is ripe and ready for romance with the dashing and erudite Robert Langdon. The irony is that the ancient Gnostics, whose books were found at Nag Hammadi, would have found this utterly repulsive. Gnosticism is a strongly ascetic religious tradition with a basic belief that spirit is good but matter, including the human body, is evil. The Gnostics of old would have denied the body and its pleasures. Brown's unwitting mixture of Gnosticism and ancient goddess worship is a gumbo that none of the old Gnostics or the old pagan practitioners of fertility religion would have found palatable. Real students of history can only wince.

Ah, but we should suspend our disbelief, shouldn't we? This is, after all, a novel! What's all the fuss about? Unfortunately, just going along for the ride could be a dangerous thing, for all too often in a postmodern situation, the public (even the church-going public) is more likely to take a novel as the gospel than the Gospels themselves. Consider for a moment those other religious bestsellers of recent years—the Left Behind series by Timothy La Haye and Jerry B. Jenkins. Indeed they are novels, but they serve up a "novel" view of end times as if it were absolutely true rather than a minority opinion within both the world of biblical scholarship and the church at large. There is much the Left Behind series has left out. Sadly, since ours is primarily an entertainment culture, we must pay close attention to the messages encoded in the entertainment lest we too become beguiled.

THE "BROWNING" OF CHRISTIAN HISTORY

Our concern is not really with Brown's mistakes about medieval history but rather the religious foundations on which his Grail theories are based. For the record, however, it is not true that the rose was primarily a symbol of the divine or sacred feminine, or of Mary Magdalene in church history. To the contrary, as the fine scholar and careful novelist Umberto Eco recognized and explored in his novel *The Name of the Rose*, the rose was a symbol of Christ, with the blood-red color symbolizing his shed blood and the thorns on the stem symbolizing his crown of thorns. Robert Langdon, the religious symbologist in *The Da Vinci Code*, should have known better, but alas he does not.

It is also highly unlikely that da Vinci's famous painting in Milan depicts Mary Magdalene sitting at the Last Supper. There was a long tradition of depicting the Beloved Disciple with fair skin and light or red hair, and it simply is not obvious that the person sitting beside Jesus in this painting is a woman. Besides, if this figure is Mary Magdalene, where is the twelfth apostle? In any case, whatever da Vinci may have had in mind tells us nothing about what actually happened at the Last Supper in A.D. 30. These errors by Brown reveal a pattern of eccentric interpretation of the sources, which carries over into the interpretation of early Christianity and the biblical sources. This should not surprise us since the main protagonist in the book ends up making a disclaimer about the pursuit of truth in such matters.

What counts most in a postmodern culture is the power of rhetoric, not the accuracy of reporting or analysis. As Robert Langdon says toward the end of the novel: "It is the mystery and wonderment that serve our souls, not the Grail itself" (p. 444). In other words, we should be content with the thrill of the chase, not the thrill of finding the truth. Langdon's comment is a strange remark in a book that repeatedly insists the world deserves the *truth* about the church's "lies" about Jesus, Mary Magdalene and the Grail (see pp. 407-8).

Robert Langdon, the hero of the book, says:

> *Every* faith in the world is based on fabrication. That is the definition of *faith*—acceptance of that which we imagine to be true, that which we cannot prove. Every religion describes God through metaphor, allegory, and exaggeration. . . . The problems arise when we begin to believe literally in our own metaphors. . . . Those who truly understand their faiths understand the stories are metaphorical. (pp. 341-42)

Philosophical claims like these undergird much of what is found in this novel, and it's not surprising that this leads to some clear errors of fact and of interpretation of key historical matters. We will deal with this philosophical and religious mishmash in due course, but first a short tour of the seven deadly historical errors of the book

Error 1. The canonical Gospels (Matthew, Mark, Luke and John) are not the earliest Gospels; rather the earliest are the suppressed Gnostic Gospels (*such as the* Gospel of Philip *or the* Gospel of Mary). This claim is made more than once by the protagonists of the book, Teabing and Langdon. They claim that the four canonical Gospels were chosen from among some eighty Gospels, and the rest were suppressed (see p. 231). In fact, there were less than twenty documents that might be called Gospels (telling the story of Jesus' life), and of those Brown's book depends on, the *Gospel of Philip* and the *Gospel of Mary*, there is no credible evidence that they existed before or during the time that the New Testament Gospels were written. The

Gnostic Gospels were written late in the second century or even the third century A.D.

No scholars that I know, whatever their theological persuasion, think that the canonical Gospels are from any later than the last half of the first century A.D. (or possibly in the case of John's Gospel, the first few years of the second century). Since Gnostic thought only came to the fore in the middle and later parts of the second century A.D., it's not surprising that the *Gospel of Philip* and the *Gospel of Mary* did not arise earlier.

One of the key indicators that Gnosticism is a later development is its dependence on the canonical Gospels for its substance when it comes to the story of Jesus. Even more tellingly Gnosticism tries to de-Judaize the story. By this I mean Gnosticism reflects a belief about the material world that does not fit well with the Old or the New Testaments, both of which affirm the goodness of God's creation. Gnosticism by contrast sees spirit as good and matter, including the body and sexual activity, as inherently tainted and evil.

Dan Brown seems to be oblivious to this fact when he draws on the Gnostic Gospels. He seems to confuse the Gnostic perspective with the sort of paganism that affirms not merely the goodness but the sacredness of sex as a way to get in touch with the "sacred feminine." This is far from the perspective of the Gnostic Gospels. Nevertheless, his protagonist calls these Gospels "the unaltered gospels" (p. 248). As a rule of thumb, the more esoteric and less Jewish a Gospel, the less likely it reflects the earliest stages of the Gospel tradition. The Gnostic Gospels reflect a nonbiblical theology that devalues the goodness of the material creation.

Error 2. Jesus is a great man or prophet in the earliest historical sources but was later proclaimed divine at the Council of Nicaea (pp. 231-34). This is patently false. Jesus is called "God" *(theos)* some seven times in the New Testament, including in the Gospel of John, and he is called "Lord" *(kyrios)* in the divine sense numerous times as well. No historian I know of argues that these New Testament texts postdate the Council of Nicaea. The documents written in the first century about Jesus and his movement suggest he was the divine Son of God. The Council of Nicaea in the fourth century and the Council of Chalcedon in the fifth century merely formalized these beliefs in creeds and sought to clarify (1) the relationship of Christ to God the Father and (2) the relationship of Christ's human and divine natures. These were not ideas conjured up by either of these councils.

Error 3. Emperor Constantine suppressed the "earlier" Gnostic Gospels and imposed the canonical Gospels and the doctrine of the divinity of Christ on the church. It is simply not true that the Gnostic Gospels were suppressed during the period when they arose. They were never recognized as authoritative in either the Eastern or Western church. Lack of recognition is not the same as suppression. The four biblical Gospels, as well as Paul's letters, were recognized as sacred and authoritative tradition by A.D. 130, long before Constantine was born. Irenaeus reports that these four Gospels were circulating together as authoritative sources in the church as early as the first half of the second century A.D. In addition, we also have the witness of the Muratorian Canon (a list of Christian books from the late second century), which names the four Gospels as authoritative in and for the church.

Constantine did not become sole emperor in the West until 312 and did not convene the Council of Nicaea until 325, shortly after his conquest of the Eastern provinces. Though he presided over the council, there is no reason to believe he shaped its conclusions, which represented the consensus of bishops throughout the entire church. The council's conclusions had nothing to do with the canon but only the divinity of Christ. The full canon as we now know it was recognized by A.D. 367. Constantine certainly did not engineer this canonizing process, though of course his conversion to Christianity helped the new faith to spread.

Error 4. Jesus was married to Mary Magdalene. Since the New Testament is completely silent on this matter and does not even indirectly support these ideas, the books protagonists turn to other and later sources for information, in particular the *Gospel of Philip,* probably written sometime in the late third century A.D. Unfortunately, the relevant portion of this text has gaps. Thus it reads: "And the companion of the [. . .] Mary Magdalene. [. . . loved] her more than [all] the disciples [and used to] kiss her [often] on her [. . .]" (the bracketed portions reflect gaps in the manuscript). In *The Da Vinci Code* the protagonist Teabing argues that in the *Gospel of Philip* the word *companion* means "spouse." However, if the text is referring to a relationship Jesus had with Mary Magdalene, it certainly isn't evident that it was a marital relationship. Indeed the context suggests it was a spiritual relationship.

What about the kiss? A parallel passage in the *Gospel of Philip* 58, 30–59, 4 seems to suggest a kiss on the mouth. But, as Karen King says in *The Gospel of Mary of Magdala*, it most likely was a chaste kiss of fellowship. The so-called holy kiss referred to in Paul's own letters (see the end of 1 Corinthians 16) is in all likelihood meant here. What makes this especially likely is that this is a Gnostic document, where human sexual expression is seen as defiling. We will examine these issues in more detail in chapter two.

Error 5. Jesus must have been married since he was an early Jew (p. 245). This argument overlooks the fact that there were already exceptions to this sort of rule in early Judaism. Ancient Jewish authors attest to the fact that some early Jews were called to celibacy. There is no reason why Jesus could not have been one of them.

In fact, it would appear that Jesus' cousin John the Baptist set such a precedent for this kin group, and there were earlier prophetic figures (Elijah, perhaps) who may also have remained single. Many scholars, probably rightly, see Matthew 19:10-12 as Jesus' own justification for remaining single. The kingdom was coming, and it was appropriate for either he or his disciples to remain single in order to focus on their ministry. If this conclusion is correct, then the later medieval conjecture about the marriage of Mary Magdalene and Jesus (and their supposed descendants) is completely discredited.

Error 6. The Dead Sea Scrolls along with the Nag Hammadi documents are the earliest Christian records (pp. 234, 245). This is so false it's what the British would call a howler. The Dead Sea Scrolls are purely Jewish documents; there is nothing Christian about them. There is also no evidence any of the Nag Hammadi documents existed before the late second century A.D., with the possible exception of the *Gospel of Thomas*.

Error 7. Thus far we have examined some historical errors in Dan Brown's book, but we also need to look at some of the philosophical and theological underpinnings of the novel. Whatever he or others may think about the theological beliefs of early Christians, it is wrong to misrepresent that belief system. At one juncture in *The Da Vinci Code*, Teabing argues that the church had to suppress the notion that Jesus was married because "a child of Jesus would undermine the critical notion of Christ's divinity and therefore the Christian Church" (p. 254). What seems to underlie this contention is the false notion that if Jesus had sexual relationships with a wife and sired offspring it would be defiling, or perhaps that as a divine being, Jesus couldn't also be fully human. This of course is not what the creeds suggest. They affirm that Jesus was both fully human as well as fully divine.

Quite simply, there is no reason why Jesus could not have been married. Since Jesus did not teach that sex was defiling (indeed, in Mark 10:1-12, he speaks of it as the means by which two become one flesh as God intended), there is no reason why a married Jesus could not have had sexual relationships and even offspring. Clearly Mark 9–10 reveal that Jesus loved children. Later Christian and Gnostic ascetics had problems with these things, but not Jesus.

At a more philosophical level there are some very significant problems with Brown's book. He apparently fails to grasp that early Christianity, like early Judaism, is not primarily about symbols and metaphors but is deeply rooted in history, including events like the exodus, the reign of King David and the life, death and resurrection of Jesus.

Of course, truth sometimes is expressed through symbol and metaphor, such as in Jesus' parables. But the Gospels themselves are not mere allegories or symbolic myths; they are ancient biographies written according to the historical and literary conventions of the time. They are based, as Luke 1:1-4 says, on the reports of eyewitnesses to these historical events. Christian faith, like Jewish faith, is not engendered by cleverly devised fables or wish fulfillment. It would be hard to imagine, for instance, ancient Jews, Jesus' disciples, making up a story about a virginal birth when that wasn't how they understood the prophecy of the coming Messiah (Isaiah 7:14). Indeed, Jesus' unusual birth suggested to the skeptical that Jesus was illegitimate, a notion not congenial to the idea he was the Messiah. No, Christianity is based on certain irreducible and irreplaceable historical events that are the foundation of the faith.

In the end and at the most profound level, Brown misjudges the biblical portrayal of the character of God. He keeps referring to the repression of the "sacred feminine." He contends that this can be found in the Old Testament, suggesting that the Shekinah glory (the physical manifestation of God's presence) originally was seen as a female deity (see p. 309). The problem with this is that God is neither male nor female in the Bible. Rather God, the Creator God, is Spirit (see John 4:24).

The Bible does not attempt to replace ancient female deities with one or more males. People of the Greco-Roman world believed in many gods and goddesses. Jews and later Christians were a tiny minority swimming against the religious current of that world, and they insisted that there is only one God, who is Spirit. This God is not a mere participant in the reproductive cycle of life, like the gods of the crops (Baal) or the fertility goddesses (Magna Mater). On the contrary, he is the One who created all life and indeed the whole material universe. No one can be united with the God of the Bible through sacred sex. Indeed no self-chosen human process could divinize human beings. Eternal life is a gift of God to his people, not an achievement or a self-induced experience. It is no more appropriate to talk about the "sacred feminine" than it is to talk about the "sacred masculine." Human beings are created in the image of God, which means they are created with a unique capacity among creatures for a full, personal relationship with God. In the Bible, being born is seen as very good thing, being born again, even better, but the latter is not achieved by sexual expression.

In Shakespeare's King Henry IV, Part Two, the king rebukes Prince Hal, who is contemplating his father's death and his own assumption of the throne, saying, "Have you a ruffian that will . . . commit the oldest sins the newest kind of ways?" There really is nothing very new about the religious agendas underlying *The Da Vinci Code*. It is simply a bad amalgam of old paganism and, strangely enough, old Gnosticism brought back to life by a masterful storyteller. It can be quite entertaining but also misleading. We need to treat this book as what it really is—not historical fiction but almost entirely fiction, at least when it comes to its assumptions and assertions about Jesus, Mary Magdalene and early Christianity. As beguiling as the thrill of the chase is, it can't hold a candle to the thrill of finding the truth about things that have shaped the very contours of history.

TWO

NO WEDDINGS AND A FUNERAL

E veryone loves a wedding, and what could be more spectacular than finding an account of Jesus' Jewish wedding! *Holy Blood, Holy Grail* floats the idea that the wedding feast of Cana, recounted in John 2, is really the story of Jesus' own wedding—even though the story itself never claims this. In this chapter we will explore the claim that Jesus was married. The most important thing about this claim is that it is almost entirely an argument from silence since no source of any kind directly says that Jesus was married, not even the Gnostic Gospels.

JESUS—THE BRIDEGROOM WHO NEVER MARRIED

The story of the wedding in Cana (John 2:1-12) begins by telling us that Jesus' mother was at the wedding. This is an odd and indeed superfluous way to begin if this was Jesus' wedding. Then we are told that Jesus and his disciples were also invited to the wedding. This makes it perfectly clear that this can't be Jesus' own wedding. The host of a wedding banquet is not invited to his own wedding feast, and we know that in early Judaism the wedding banquet was held at the home of the bridegroom or his father (see Matthew 22:1-14; 25:1-13). In neither case was an invitation to the groom required or in order.

Next we are informed that Mary comes to Jesus and says, "they have no wine." The *they* must surely be the wedding party, in particular the bride and groom. In an honor-and-shame culture this would be a terribly shameful mistake, for the groom and his family were responsible for making sure the festivities were properly planned, prepared and administered. Jesus' response to the implied request of Mary is, "What concern is that to you and to me?" This is an unimaginable response if Jesus was in fact obligated as the groom to do something about this problem. Nevertheless, Jesus miraculously provides the wine.

We are told in verses 9-10 that the "toastmaster," not knowing about Jesus' miracle, called the groom aside and commented that the best wine had been saved till the last. Once again, this reveals that the bridegroom is responsible for the management of the feast, and Jesus is not that bridegroom. (The latter is not identified by name.) The coup de grâce to the theory that this is Jesus' own wedding is that verse 12 reports that Jesus left the wedding and went off with his mother, brothers and disciples—but not his supposed wife! There is no positive evidence here that Jesus is married, and indeed there is confirmation that this story is not about Jesus' own wedding. There are no other texts in the canonical Gospels that even hint that Jesus might have been married.

What was Jesus' own view of marriage? It can be summed up as follows—one life, one wife. When we examine Mark 10 (and its parallel text in Matthew 19) a variety of important things come to light. First, Jesus' teaching on divorce clearly seems to be stricter than other early Jewish teachers. Jesus' basic view seems to be that there should be no divorce for those God has joined together. Mark 10, our earliest source on Jesus' teaching on this matter, suggests this conclusion, which is confirmed in 1 Corinthians 7:10-11, where Paul says Jesus taught that even if a married couple had separated, divorce was not to follow. The reason for this teaching seems to be that Jesus thought that the one-flesh union of husband and wife created a permanent bond as long as they both lived. This is why Jesus warns in Mark 10 and Matthew 19 that the man who divorces his wife and marries another has committed adultery against his first wife. This assumes that the first union was still in effect.

In Matthew's Gospel the disciples protest Jesus' declaration and say that if divorce is never right, then it's better for a man not to marry. In that culture women could be divorced, but they didn't have the right to initiate divorce. Jesus' teaching is striking in many regards, and its net effect was to give women more security in marriage. And in Matthew 19:10-12 he proposes an alternative. Jesus says that his disciples can remain single for the sake of the kingdom. Now it is interesting that his disciples don't protest this suggestion as they had the "no divorce" rule. Nonetheless, this teaching was unconventional and unusual in early Judaism.

Early Jews seem to have believed that the command in Genesis to "be fruitful and multiply" was a requirement for all able-bodied persons. Thus there needed to be a special rationale for not doing so. Jesus provides a rationale in Matthew 19:10-12. He says, not surprisingly, that those who are born eunuchs are not obligated to marry and have children. But the next two categories would have caused some surprise—Jesus speaks of those who are made eunuchs and those who make themselves eunuchs. Jews, in general, did not practice what other Semitic cultures did, namely, making certain males into eunuchs to guard the harem or the treasury. And the idea of a man making himself a eunuch would have been particularly repugnant to Jews. It is likely, however, that Jesus meant this to be taken metaphorically, that is, as a dedication to remaining single rather than actual self-castration.

Because of this passage various New Testament scholars have concluded that Jesus was an ascetic. Remaining single for the sake of the kingdom, however, is not identical with being an ascetic. It's perfectly clear that in this same passage Jesus affirmed marriage and having children (on children, see also Mark 9–10). Jesus' view that God's final saving activity was happening during his ministry didn't prevent him from affirming marriage, even for his own inner circle of disciples. Nevertheless, this passage is Jesus' rationale for why he chose to remain single. The kingdom of God was breaking into human history, and Jesus' ministry required his single-minded devotion.

One further consideration is important. There are various texts in the New Testament Gospels that suggest Jesus realized he was facing a premature funeral. In Mark 8–10 there are no less than four Passion predictions—

the Son of Man must suffer many things, be killed and on the third day arise. In view of how controversial some of Jesus' actions and words were, it would not take a rocket scientist to realize that he would face a premature death. Under these circumstances it is perfectly understandable that Jesus would have chosen to abstain from marriage.

As unusual as it might have been, it wasn't unprecedented for an early Jewish leader or a particularly devout Jew to abstain from marriage for some religious purpose. Archaeological explorations near the Dead Sea have shown that there were both married and single men and women in the Qumran community. The community there, perhaps especially because of their belief that the end of days was near, made room for a commitment to celibacy among its members. Jesus did likewise. But there is more evidence of celibacy within early Judaism. The two most prominent non-Christian Jewish writers from the New Testament era, Josephus and Philo, both refer to celibate Jews during this time.

Furthermore, various prophetic figures likely remained single in earlier Jewish eras. Elijah appears without family in 1-2 Kings and is taken up into heaven at the close of his ministry. Hosea had to be told by God to take Gomer as a wife. John the Baptist clearly was an ascetic, both in terms of diet and relationships. There is no reason why Jesus could not likewise have abstained from marriage and sexual relations. The case that Jesus was married because early Jews invariably got married, as W. E. Phipps contends in *Was Jesus Married?* has been greatly overstated. It doesn't take into account the callings of prophets and other holy or exceptional persons.

Jesus however did not mandate celibacy, as is perfectly clear from an aside made by Paul: "Do we not have the right to be accompanied by a believing wife, *as do the other apostles and the brothers of the Lord and Cephas?*" (1 Corinthians 9:5, italics added). Here Paul certainly would have mentioned the example of Jesus being married had it been so. In fact this text is the earliest statement on the marital status of any member of Jesus' family. (In all likelihood, the Gospels were written well after Paul's letters.) Paul assumes his audience knows perfectly well that neither he nor Jesus were married.

Why then did Jesus use the dramatic metaphor about being a eunuch for the sake of the kingdom instead of just talking about being single or remaining unmarried? The answer to this is important. A eunuch is a person who does not, indeed cannot, engage in sexual relationships for some reason. If the person is a literal eunuch, the reason is obvious. But if this refers to a personal commitment, then he is referring to the choice to abstain from sexual relationships while not married. In other words, Jesus' teaching in Matthew 19 is that fidelity in marriage and celibacy in singleness is what Jesus' disciples should see as their only legitimate options.

This in turn rules out the notion that Jesus might have sired a child prior to or outside of a marriage. In this honor-and-shame culture and with his calling to ministry, it is unthinkable that Jesus would have considered such an option. So we see that the New Testament does not support the suggestion that Jesus was married or had children. But what about the literature outside the Bible, including the Gnostic Gospels? Before we turn to these documents, it is important to state a crucial principle of historical study: *It is always more likely that those sources that come from eyewitnesses or those who were in contact with eyewitnesses will provide us with the best data about an ancient person than documents that were composed several centuries later, as were the Gnostic Gospels.* There would need to be clear and compelling evidence corroborated by several later sources for us to take the word of later documents that Jesus was married. There is no such evidence, even in the Gnostic Gospels.

GNOSTIC KNOWLEDGE OF JESUS

The Nag Hammadi documents were discovered in the desert of Egypt in 1945. The documents are thirteen leather-bound books written in Coptic (not Aramaic as a character in *The Da Vinci Code* claims). In the *Anchor Bible Dictionary* Gary Lease and Birger Pearson say: "The codices date to the 4th century and reflect a combination of gnostic and Christian elements." By 1977 these codices had been carefully examined, and all were published both in the original language and in English translation. Notice

how Pearson, a fine scholar, implies in the quotation that there is a difference between mainstream Christian thought and Gnosticism. He is absolutely correct.

Gnostic documents represent neither the earliest nor most authentic
materials about Jesus and his followers. Indeed they represent a departure
from early materials in various ways, including their theology of creation
and redemption. Gnosticism was not only out of line with mainstream
Christianity, it was also out of line with Judaism as well.

Of particular concern are the *Gospel of Philip* (written in Coptic) and
the *Gospel of Mary* (which first appears in a Coptic edition and later a
Greek edition, though only fragments have been recovered). Do either of
these documents lead us to believe, as the protagonists in *The Da Vinci
Code* claim, that (1) Jesus was married, and (2) he was married to Mary
Magdalene?

In fact, the very character of these documents make it quite unlikely that
they affirm such a thing, for Gnosticism was strongly ascetic, meaning, in
part, that it would have discouraged marriage. Furthermore, neither the
Gospel of Philip nor the *Gospel of Mary* are Gospels at all if by *Gospel* we
mean a public commentary on the life and ministry of the earthly Jesus.
The *Gospel of Philip* is an anthology of esoteric lore culled from other documents, and the *Gospel of Mary* falls under the category of apocalypse
rather than Gospel. Gnosticism was based on secret spiritual truths that the
risen Jesus supposedly revealed to a very select circle of disciples, including
Mary Magdalene. Salvation depended on whether a person had this secret
knowledge.

Not surprisingly, these documents have little interest in Jesus' earthly relationships and activities. The Gnostics believed an elite group had direct
access to knowledge that other Christians didn't have. Basically they believed that with this secret knowledge the light of God opens certain disciples' eyes to the light that dwells within them. With this insider knowledge
of the soul's origin in and close union with God, a person is freed and so
saved. Thus in *The Gnostic Gospels* Elaine Pagels correctly observes that for

the Gnostics "theology is really anthropology"—that is, revelation is about the human self, and salvation is found within the self. As Darrell Bock notes in his recent book *Breaking the Da Vinci Code*, the major subject of this literature is the inner self, not God, and the major spiritual problem is perceived to be lack of knowledge, not sin.

For example, here is a not-so-controversial text found in the *Gospel of Mary*:

> But Andrew answered and said to the brethren, "Say what you (wish to) say about what she has said. I at least do not believe that the Savior said this. For certainly these teachings are strange ideas." Peter answered and spoke concerning these same things. He questioned them about the Savior: "Did he really speak with a woman without our knowledge (and) not openly? Are we to turn about and all listen to her? Did he prefer her to us?"
>
> Then Mary wept and said to Peter, "My brother Peter, what do you think? Do you think that I thought this up myself in my heart, or that I am lying about the Savior?" Levi answered and said to Peter, "Peter you have always been hot-tempered. Now I see you contending against the woman like the adversaries. But if the Savior made her worthy, who are you indeed to reject her? Surely the Savior knows her very well. That is why he loved her more than us. Rather let us be ashamed and put on the perfect man and acquire him for ourselves as he commanded us, and preach the gospel, not laying down any other rule or other law beyond what the Savior said."

This text, like others in this so-called Gospel, comes out of reflection on and development of ideas found in the Gospel of John, in particular John 20, where Jesus appears first to Mary Magdalene and commissions her to tell the good news to the remaining eleven disciples. In particular the *Gospel of Mary* here is referring to a special revelation that came to Mary from Jesus, which set her apart from the male disciples and, in this story, led to jealousy and rancor. Mary's word is not believed, apparently chiefly because she is a woman, and these disciples cannot understand why Jesus might honor her with a first appearance and revelation rather than them.

It may well be that texts like these were created because there was a struggle in Gnostic Christianity between male and female teachers, and texts like this were written either to support or supplant women teachers. Be that as it may, this episode does not correspond with anything that is found in canonical Gospels, which predate A.D. 150. (The *Gospel of Mary* was created at the earliest at the end of the second century A.D.) This text may suggest a tradition in which Mary Magdalene was conjectured to be the Beloved Disciple, since Levi declares "he loved her more than us." (This idea, of course, is contrary to what we find in John 19, where both the Beloved Disciple and Mary Magdalene are said to be standing beneath the cross.) In any case, the context of this story shows clearly that what is being discussed here is Jesus' love for his disciples, not some male-female intimacy between Jesus and Mary Magdalene. The comparison of the degree of love makes clear that the author is referring to a love Jesus might have for either male or female disciples. There is certainly nothing here that supports the notion that Jesus was married, much less that he was married to Mary Magdalene.

There is more to be said about the context of this quotation. Mary claims to have received this revelation in a vision of Jesus, and it is interesting that the first reaction of one of the male disciples, Andrew, is as follows: "Tell me, what do you think of these things she has been telling us? As for me, I do not believe that the Teacher would speak like this. *These ideas are too different from those we have known.*" This remark is telling because it shows that the author of this document is well aware of the reaction of the orthodox church to such ideas. It anticipates an objection and then answers it by another male disciple, in this case Levi.

The text of this document is very brief, and clearly there are absolutely no statements in this document that identify Mary Magdalene as or with the "sacred feminine" concept of Wisdom. This is a figment of the imagination. We won't find such a notion in the *Gospel of Philip* either. Mary is simply identified as one of the disciples who has had a vision of Jesus and exhorts the male disciples on the basis of it. Only humans have visions, not divine beings. Furthermore she includes herself as among those who need to become male or, as Jean-Yves Leloup insists on translating it, "fully human." Mary is a disciple who has had a vision and shares the secret wisdom she has received. She is not Wisdom originating the secrets she is passing along.

More controversial and unfortunately more fragmentary is the Coptic text of the *Gospel of Philip* 63,32-36, which reads at the key juncture: "And the companion of the [. . .] Mary Magdalene. [. . . loved] her more than [all] the disciples [and used to] kiss her [often] on her [. . .]." (Again, this text is damaged and the bracketed portions reflect gaps in the manuscript, into which scholars have inserted various conjectures.) We will deal first with the key term that begins the passage—*companion*. Strictly speaking we are not told *who* Mary Magdalene was the companion of, but the assumption of most scholars is that it must be Jesus. In *The Da Vinci Code* Teabing argues that in the *Gospel of Philip* the word *companion* means "spouse" because that's what the Aramaic word means (p. 246). Unfortunately, this document was not written in Aramaic. Like the other Nag Hammadi documents, it was written in Coptic. The word here for "companion" *(koinōnos)* is actually a loan word from Greek that is neither a technical term nor a synonym for "wife" or "spouse." It's true the term could include the idea that the woman was a wife, since *koinōnos* is an umbrella term, but it doesn't specify this fact. There was another Greek word, *gynē*, that would have made this clearer. But in fact it's much more likely that *koinōnos* here means "sister" in the spiritual sense; this is how it is used elsewhere in this sort of literature. The important point is that even this text doesn't clearly say or even suggest that Jesus was married at all, much less married to Mary Magdalene.

The other conundrum about this text is Mary Magdalene's kiss. In view of the text we looked at before from the *Gospel of Mary*, the phrase "[. . . loved] her more than [all] the disciples" probably means that this is about the relationship between Mary Magdalene and Jesus. It's possible to fill in the actual gap in the manuscript—"kiss her [. . .] on her [. . .]"—with the

Coptic words for *head* or *hand* or *cheek* or *mouth*. We may have a clue to what is meant from another passage in the *Gospel of Philip*: "For it is by a kiss that the perfect conceive and give birth. For this reason we also kiss one another. We receive conception from the grace which is in one another."

Even Karen King argues that what is referred to here is clearly asexual — a holy kiss or kiss of fellowship between believers. In my judgment the key to understanding the quoted text is to note that the aim of such kissing is spiritual birth or rebirth. Genital sex is avoided but holy kisses are allowed because what really matters is spiritual reproduction, not fleshly reproduction. The context of this material is clearly ascetic, which is in keeping with Gnostic literature in general.

The author of the *Gospel of Mary* would likely be horrified by the suggestion that Jesus had a sexual or normal marital relationship with Mary. Notice that the text insists "for this reason we all kiss one another." Intimacy is implied, and it involves all the disciples, both male and female. It's a spiritual intimacy that all disciples could share with one another, just as Jesus shared with Mary. In short, there is nothing here to support the theory that Jesus was married to Mary Magdalene or anyone else. That would require a non-Gnostic reading of this passage, taking it out of its Gnostic and ascetic context. This is, of course, precisely what Dan Brown's fictional scholars do in *The Da Vinci Code* (pp. 246-48). Indeed, the word *mouth* is added to the translation of the *Gospel of Philip* passage to help make their case. But in fact we don't know for sure what word belongs there.

JESUS, THE UNMARRIED BRIDEGROOM

To conclude, nothing in the biblical Gospels or in the Gnostic Gospels suggests that Jesus was married, much less married to Mary Magdalene. Only when people take texts out of their context and read them with a modern agenda could they come to such a conclusion. Gnostic Gospels should be read with a very critical eye when it comes to historical claims. These Gospels are dated so much later than the biblical Gospels and are pushing Gnostic agendas that the historical Jesus knew nothing of.

THREE

TELL ME THE OLD, OLD STORY

I t's no fun to come in on the middle of a movie you have not seen before or to begin reading The Lord of the Rings series at the second volume, *The Two Towers*. So, where should we start when interpreting Jesus and early Christianity? And whose stories should we primarily listen to? In this chapter we will examine the claim in *The Da Vinci Code* that the biblical Gospels are not the earliest Gospels, but the Gnostic Gospels are (p. 248).

To begin, even the vast majority of scholars who highly value the Gnostic Gospels know they aren't the earliest Gospels. Sometimes they do indulge in theories that the biblical Gospels have repressed, silenced or hidden the roles of women. Not much stock should be put in such arguments, for they are arguments from silence. In fact the New Testament offers a very high view of women and their roles as teachers, preachers, prophets, patrons, deacons, apostles, house-church leaders and a host of other roles in early Christianity. This includes the roles that Mary Magdalene played.

The vast majority of scholars recognize the biblical Gospels to be the earliest Gospel documents. Though it is certainly true that the same critical scrutiny should be applied to these Gospels that is applied to sources outside the Bible, most scholars have recognized that these documents, and not the much later Gnostic Gospels, provide us with the best opportunity to learn things about both the historical Jesus and the early Christian use of the Gospels.

THE MEANING OF GOSPEL

The term *gospel* comes to us from the Old English term *godspel*, meaning

"good story" or "good news," a direct translation of the late Latin term *evangelium*. *Evangelium* is the Latin transliteration of the Greek
euangelion, which again means "good news."
We are so familiar with the religious use of the
term *gospel* that we have forgotten, or perhaps
have never heard, that *euangelion* was a common and widely used term in ancient times.
Indeed, it was even used of good news about
the birth and deeds of the Roman emperor before it was ever used of Jesus. Furthermore, it
is unlikely that the term *euangelion* was already a technical term for a particular kind of
literature by the time Mark wrote his work. To
the ancients what we know as the Gospels
would have seemed much like other ancient
historical or biographical works, only in this
case about a religious figure. Significantly, by
the last decade of the first century A.D. (or the
early decades of the second century) references are made to written documents called
"Gospels" in the early Christian document
called the *Didache*. In other words, this confirms that these works were composed and circulated before the end of the first century A.D.
It also confirms that the term *Gospel* was beginning to be associated with a particular type
of Christian literature—the story of Jesus' life
and ministry. The *Didache*, an early manual
of church instruction, shows particular famil-
iarity with Matthew, but the author seems to
know other biblical Gospels as well.

GOSPEL SOURCES

Q—from the German Quelle
("source"). Q refers to material found in both Matthew
and Luke but not in Mark. It
is chiefly composed of sayings of Jesus, but some narratives are included (for example, the temptations of
Jesus). We have no manu-
scripts of Q; scholars debate
whether this source ever existed as a written document
and, if so, what exactly it did
or didn't contain.

M—stands for the special
source of material found
only in the Gospel of Matthew (for example, the birth
narratives).

L—stands for the special
source of material found
only in the Gospel of Luke
(for example, the parable of
the good Samaritan).

The usual solution to the
problem of what sources
were used in composing the
Gospels of Matthew, Mark
and Luke is that Mark wrote
first, and the First and Third
Evangelists used Mark and
other sources: Q and M in the
case of Matthew and Q and L
in the case of Luke.

What then are the Gospels? They are documents about Jesus that drew on pre-Gospel sources in the process of composition. Furthermore, three of these documents have a close literary relationship, leading to the likely conclusion that Mark was written first. Subsequently Mark was used to compose the Gospels of Matthew and Luke. These two Gospel writers also used a common sayings source, which today is called Q, and other distinctive sources, called "M" in the case of Matthew and "L" in the case of Luke. But what are we to make of the finished products? Again, what are the Gospels? In my view three of the Gospels—Matthew, Mark and John—appear to be ancient biographies, while the Luke-Acts combination appears to be an ancient two-volume historical monograph. I will explore these possibilities further, one Gospel at a time. First, however, see the "Gospel Sources" sidebar (p. 39), which will help you to decipher the scholarly language about sources of Gospel material.

THE GOSPEL OF MARK

We need to keep in mind that certain features of ancient biographies are also found in ancient historical monographs. The basic difference is that a biography focuses on a single person and recounts revealing stories about the person's character or nature (whether the events were of historic significance or not). Historical monographs by contrast focus on events and the flow of cause and effect, and are seldom interested in personal anecdotes that are not of any historic significance.

In general, Mark's Gospel shows only a little interest in historical causality. Apart from the Passion narrative, Mark makes little attempt to link one event to the next or one story to another. He selectively presents episodes in the life of Jesus. Mark also shows no interest in linking world events and the Gospel stories. People are mentioned in Mark's narrative only because of their connection, direct or indirect, with Mark's central character, Jesus. This is true even of major figures like Peter, John the Baptist and Caiaphas, the high priest. In addition, the way the disciples and crowds are presented in Mark suggests that the author has an ethical agenda: he wants his audience to follow or avoid certain examples. This fits ancient biographical works like Plutarch's famous *Parallel Lives* far better than it does ancient historical monographs.

Mark's Gospel is written in Greek, though there is evidence that the author knows some Aramaic, Hebrew and Latin. It was written well after the rise of both the Greek and Roman biographical traditions. The Roman biography, which came to the fore in the first century A.D., is especially germane for our investigation because it adds certain features to its adaptation of the Greek tradition: there is a greater concern for family traditions and sometimes, most tellingly, a focus on the hero's patient suffering and death at the hands of some tyrant (see, for example, Thraesa Paetus's *Life of Cato*). These sorts of biographies were especially in vogue during the reigns of Nero and Domitian. In other words, the Gospels were written when people were sympathetic to hearing the story of a virtuous man who suffered unjustly and had an untimely demise. It's not accidental that the Gospels have been called Passion narratives with long introductions. Some 19 percent of Mark's Gospel is devoted to the Passion narrative, while John's account devotes more than 40 percent to the events of the last week of Jesus' life.

There are indicators that Mark, Matthew and John are biographies. First, they all introduce their main protagonists at the beginning of the document, whereas in Luke's Gospel Jesus does not come to the fore until after Luke 1. (Thus an ancient person reading the beginning of Luke's scroll would not have recognized it to be a biography of Jesus.) Second, these documents are the right length to fit on an ancient scroll. Even at a glance all three documents are some sort of prose narrative or story; they are not plays, speeches or the like. In Mark's Gospel, Jesus is the subject of over 44 percent of all the verbs.

Mark, Matthew and John follow the convention of indirect portraiture; they let the deeds and words of Jesus speak for themselves without much analysis or additional comment. Mark and Matthew follow the rhetorical convention of using short, pithy narratives that conclude with a dramatic pronouncement or memorable deed. John's Gospel offers monologues and dialogues, and more closely resembles the life of a philosopher or sage than the life of a prophet or preacher. All three Gospels, however, go out of their way to portray Jesus as both a proclaimer-teacher and a healer.

Biographies were popular literature in the first century A.D. They were not necessarily for a highbrow audience; they could be read aloud to groups profitably, containing as they did selected short episodes from a life. They did not compete with classics like Homer's *Odyssey* or Virgil's *Aeneid* in terms of literary merit or sophistication. Historical monographs, by contrast, tended to be for the well-educated—the movers and shakers in society who were both literate and involved in major social and civic affairs. That Luke-Acts appears more like the historical monologues of Thucydides or Polybius than Plutarch's *Lives* must surely tell us something about Luke's audience.

A few of the conventions of ancient biographies need to be kept in mind. First, these were never exhaustive accounts of a person's life. The limitations of scrolls and of the means of researching and writing prohibited anything that might be comparable to a modern biography. Second, ancient biographies were not written in the post-Freudian, post-Jungian era. That is, they did not operate with modern developmental personality models. Most ancients seemed to believe that a person was born and stuck with the personality he or she had, and that personality was eventually revealed over time, not developed. They also believed that how a person died most revealed his or her character, which is the very reason why the Gospel writers had to explain in detail the demise of their hero, Jesus. He died in the least honorable way possible. How could this be explained if he was a virtuous man? In the Roman tradition there was an answer to this question, as the *Lives of Julius Caesar* shows. Death revealed also what God or the gods thought of a person. The Passion narratives had to come to grips with this basic ancient assumption. Third, ancient biographies don't spend much time on a person's youth. Normally, the focus is on the adult life. This is the case in all three of the more biographical Gospels, although Matthew and John do speak briefly about the antecedents to Jesus' adult life. Fourth, ancient biographies weren't all that concerned with the physical appearance of the person in question (unless it was particularly striking). The biographies of Jesus are no different in this regard. Fifth, ancient biographies were not greatly concerned about either precise chronology or the issue of proportionality. By the latter I mean that an ancient biographer might spend an inordinate amount of time on some particular period in a person's life, not offering a balanced, womb-to-tomb portrait. Sixth, ancient biographies were certainly more like paintings than photographs. They were tendentious in character, presenting and interpreting a life from a particular point. Such writers wanted to tell the truth, but they were not laboring under the modern anxiety about objectivity.

The particulars about Mark's Gospel are both interesting and to some degree elusive. Since no one has claimed that Mark was one of the Twelve or even an eyewitness of much of Jesus' life, it seems unlikely that later church tradition would say that insignificant Mark wrote a Gospel—unless, that is, he in fact did. After all, he is only a minor figure in Acts and Paul's letters. What we do know of him is that his mother had a house in Jerusalem, and so he was based there. At one juncture Mark traveled with Paul and Barnabas. Later, apparently in the 60s, he seems to have had associations with both Paul and Peter in Rome. If, as tradition has it, Mark is the young man who fled away naked in the Passion narrative (Mark 14:51-52), then he may have been very briefly an eyewitness to some of the events at the close of Jesus' life. From Papias, a late first- to early second-century bishop, we inherit the tradition that Mark gleaned much of his material from Peter's preaching.

As for the location and time of Mark's writing, it seems to have been written for an audience of Gentile Christians in the western part of the Roman Empire, possibly Rome. There may be a clue to the dating of the book in Mark 13:14, which has the phrase "let the reader understand." This phrase suggests that Mark is writing at a time when the demise of the Jerusalem temple could be foreseen as possibly imminent. In other words, it would appear this Gospel was written sometime in A.D. 68-69, after the Jewish war was well underway but shortly before its climax in Jerusalem.

The structure of the Gospel of Mark is both simple and profound. Basically it falls into three parts and reflects something of a chronological and a theological outline. Part one comprises the first half of the Gospel, where "who" and "why" questions are raised about the identity and ministry of Jesus. The "who" question is finally answered by Peter at Caesarea Philippi (Mark 8:27-30) in a way that matches up with the beginning of the Gospel at Mark 1:1. Jesus is both Christ, or Messiah, and Son of God. After this, in three straight chapters, Mark has Jesus present the nature of his mission— he is the man who was born to die. We hear that the Son of Man must suffer many things, be killed and rise again. This way of putting the mission statement comes to a climax in Mark 10:45, where we hear that Jesus came to give his life as a ransom for many. Then, in his Passion narrative (Mark 11–16), Mark records how the mission was successfully accomplished. Mark's Gospel is also noted for having various disclosure moments, such as at the baptism and transfiguration of Jesus, which serve as a counterpoint to the messianic-secret motif found within it.

THE GOSPEL OF MATTHEW

Matthew's Gospel is a composite of several known sources, including 95 percent of Mark, a wide range of Q material and the unique M material (such as what we find in the birth narratives). But why would one of the original twelve disciples, who was an eyewitness to the life of Jesus, be so dependent on a Gospel written by someone who was not an eyewitness? This question is why most scholars don't think Matthew the tax collector wrote the First Gospel. It is quite possible, however, that Matthew contributed the unique material found in this Gospel, and therefore the book came to be named after its most famous contributor, which was not uncommon in antiquity. This makes some sense of the tradition of attributing this Gospel to Matthew, which otherwise seems an odd choice since he is a minor figure among the Twelve in the Gospels. (In any case, we must remember that all four canonical Gospels are anonymous. Only later were names appended to the scrolls for identification.)

Since Matthew's Gospel is so clearly dependent on Mark, it must have been written later than Mark's Gospel, perhaps sometime in the 70s or 80s. This Gospel differs in numerous ways from Mark's Gospel, although it fits the description of being an ancient biography. Consider the following: Matthew's Gospel is the most Jewish of the Gospels; it is very concerned about the fulfillment of the Scriptures, including the law. It also emphasizes tradition and gives special focus to the teaching of Jesus, presenting us with five or six blocks of teaching material (chaps. 5-7, 10, 13, 18, 23 and 24-25), much more than we find in Mark. It is often argued that Jesus is presented as a new Moses in this Gospel, but it would be better to say that he is presented as a new Solomon, since his form of teaching is sapiential (that is, like Wisdom literature). He does not lay down the law, rather he presents the good news in a manner that is in accord with the Jewish Wisdom tradition. Picking up on hints and ideas found in Q, our Gospel writer presents Jesus as both a sage and as the embodiment of Wisdom, the very mind and presence of God on earth. There is then an understandable interest in Jesus as the Son of David, both a messianic figure and one cut in the mold of Solomon. The author of this Gospel seems to see himself as a teacher who is to bring out of his treasury both old and new wisdom (see Matthew 13:52), highlighting how Jesus can be both sage in the line of other great Davidic sages and the Wisdom of God, indeed the Son of God. Jewish kings were to be characterized by wisdom, and Jesus is the exemplar of this in Matthew's Gospel.

The Gospel of Matthew likely was written to a largely Jewish Christian audience, one that had concerns about the ongoing role of the Mosaic law in Christian life. This Gospel also highlights the role and importance of Peter in various ways, perhaps because he was the apostle to the Jews, as Galatians 2 makes evident. The overall tenor of Matthew suggests it was written at a time when the Jewish Christian community had to define itself over against the synagogue and was struggling because it was no longer sheltered under the protective umbrella of Judaism, which was a recognized religion in the Roman Empire. This consideration as well points us to a time at least in the 70s, if not later. Even so, its author wants to demonstrate that his audience has more than enough Jesus tradition to sustain their community without having to turn back to the synagogue. Jesus is the sage and master teacher. He is also the Son of David, the Son of God and even Immanuel, God's everlasting presence and Wisdom.

LUKE AND ACTS

This two-volume historical monograph probably antedates the Gospel of John by as much as twenty years. Most scholars think it is unlikely that the church would have attributed a Gospel to as minor a New Testament figure as Luke if he wasn't the real author. He was not one of the Twelve or an apostle, and he was not an eyewitness of the life of Jesus. Luke is only an occasional companion of Paul toward the end of Paul's missionary journeys. However he may have been a doctor, and so literate in his own right. Is it an accident that in his carefully crafted prologue (Luke 1:1-4) he follows the model of prologues to scientific treatises? Probably not. That prologue also tells us something else about Luke: he knows that he has predecessors and that perhaps it would be in order to do something different than what we find in Matthew or Mark or, for that matter, Q. Luke realized that a more strictly historical account following the rules for Hellenistic historiography was in order. Notice the prologue's emphasis on (1) investigating things for himself (that is, doing research), (2) examining things from the beginning (that is, backing up far enough to see where Jesus comes into the cause and effect of history), and (3) writing an orderly account. The prologue, the multiple volumes in this work, and the linking to historical events (see, for example, Luke 2:1-3; Acts 18:2) make it evident that Luke is serious about his attempt to write historical monographs that follow a careful, mostly chronological ordering of events. His work also follows the convention of dealing with materials region by region.

"Theophilus" is probably the name of Luke's patron (see Luke 1:3). Luke-Acts is as close as we come to real highbrow literature in the New

Testament. It is written primarily, if not exclusively, for a person of high social status who is apparently a recent convert and needs to have some confirmation and assurance about what he has been taught. It also includes some illumination about salvation history and Jesus and his followers' roles in it.

The structure of Luke-Acts is quite interesting. In the Gospel there is a "to Jerusalem" orientation, but in Acts we have a "from Jerusalem to the rest of the empire" orientation. In other words, there is something of a geographical as well as chronological ordering of these volumes. But Luke is interested in more than just mundane history. His interest lies in God's guiding of and interfacing with human lives and events. He wants to show how God, his Word and his Spirit are alive and active in the process of human history. It's no accident that Luke records Jesus' quotation of Isaiah (Luke 4:16-22) as a preview of coming events in Jesus' ministry. Similarly, Peter's quotation of Joel (Acts 2:14-21) foreshadows events in Acts. God has a plan for human redemption that he works out by the activities of the Word and Spirit through human lives and processes. "Salvation history" is a very apt description of what Luke records in his two-volume monograph.

Luke's Gospel chronicles how the good news spreads from Galilee to Samaria to Judea and Jerusalem, and up and down the social scale from the last, the least, and the lost to the first, the most, and the found. Jesus must go up to Jerusalem, and the disciples must wait there for power from on high before they take further action. But once Pentecost happens in Acts, Luke wants to show the spread of the good news from Jerusalem to Rome, for he is concerned to show the universal scope of the gospel to all persons, all kinds and all races of persons, no matter their social status, gender or ethnic origin. The Gospel focuses mostly on salvation up and down the social scale to all sorts and classes of people, while Acts focuses on the horizontal spread of salvation across all geographical and ethnic boundaries. Jesus is the one Savior for all peoples. Salvation comes from the Jews and from Jerusalem, but it is for everyone. God is no respecter of

persons; God is impartial. There is a special interest in the poor, oppressed, possessed and disenfranchised receiving the good news—help,
healing and salvation—but equally Luke shows how salvation also comes
to the well-to-do.

THE GOSPEL OF JOHN

As different as the Gospel of John is from the Gospel of Matthew, it nonetheless shares with Matthew a Wisdom orientation to Jesus and his teachings. Only the author of John has chosen to present Jesus as Wisdom incar-
nate, discoursing on earth as personified Wisdom does in Proverbs 8–9 and
in sources like the Wisdom of Solomon. The Fourth Evangelist does not
seem to depend on any of the earlier Gospels, though clearly he knows
some of the same Gospel traditions. Rather he pursues an independent presentation of Jesus' biography. Like the other Evangelists his presentation is
somewhat chronologically ordered, but the author is not afraid to rearrange
episodes in order to emphasize his theological agenda. (See, for example,
John 2:13-25, where we find the temple-cleansing episode, borrowed from
the Passion narrative.)

Can we know who wrote this wonderful and profound Gospel? Like the
other Gospels the document is formally anonymous, but there are clues in
John 19 and 21 that the author might be the Beloved Disciple, an eyewitness
of at least some of Jesus' ministry. John 21:24 says that the Beloved Disciple
is the one who testifies to at least some of the Gospel happenings and indeed that he wrote them down. His community vouches for his testimony
("we know his testimony is true"). John 19:35 indicates that the author of
this Gospel was present at the death of Jesus. And chapter 19 claims only
one man was present—the Beloved Disciple, to whom Jesus bequeathed
his mother as he died (verse 26).

It seems unlikely that the Fourth Gospel was written by John, son of
Zebedee. It includes only one of the Galilean miracle sequences that are in
the other three Gospels (the feeding of the five thousand and the walking
on water) and none of the episodes in which the sons of Zebedee play a sig-

nificant part. We have no story about the calling of the Zebedees to follow Jesus, nothing about their presence at the raising of Jairus's daughter or at the transfiguration, nothing about them requesting special seats in Jesus' coming kingdom and so on. Instead we find unique stories like the raising of Lazarus and the healings of the man born blind and the lame man by the pool, most of which center on Jerusalem and its environs. We also have the story in John 13 about the Beloved Disciple reclining with Jesus, and Peter having his feet washed, neither of which are mentioned in the other Gospels. Thus it seems that the Beloved Disciple, a Judean follower of Jesus, was the source of much of this material, and that he was not one of the sons of Zebedee, even though his name may have been John.

The author of this Gospel focuses so intensely on Jesus that the original twelve disciples just about disappear into the background. They are hardly ever mentioned. Unlike the other Gospels, this Gospel's Jesus isn't said to perform exorcisms and isn't presented as teaching mainly in parables. It presents us with the powerful paradox of a divine and also truly human Jesus who can say both "Before Abraham was, I am" and in the same breath indicate that he can do nothing unless his heavenly Father gives him the go ahead. The key to understanding Jesus' identity in John is knowing where he came from (from the Father, as John 1 explains) and where he is going (to the Father, as John 14–17 stress). Those who think Jesus merely has human origins or a human destiny cannot properly understand his identity.

The Gospel of John can be divided up into two major parts, a book of signs (John 2–11) and the passion and resurrection stories (John 12–20) framed by a prologue (John 1) and an epilogue (John 21). There are seven sign narratives and seven "I am" sayings and discourses. This highly schematized presentation is deliberately selective, as John 20:30 makes clear. There is something of a crescendo of the miraculous from sign one through sign seven, and the seventh sign foreshadows what will happen to Jesus in the last week of his life. There is also a crescendo of confessions, with the only one that fully matches up with the prologue's exalted view of Christ found paradoxically on the lips of Thomas, who when he sees the risen

Jesus proclaims, "My Lord and my God" (which is, not coincidentally, also what Emperor Domitian asked to be called). This provides a clue that this Gospel was written at a time when the emperor cult was strong and Domitian was its focus. This in turn means that the Gospel of John was likely finally assembled in the 90s, though its traditions from the Beloved Disciple may go much further back.

The author of John goes out of his way to shed light, indeed glory, on the cross. The cross in this Gospel is seen as the first stage of Jesus' exaltation. When Jesus is lifted up on the cross, he draws all persons to himself. Furthermore, there is no agony on the cross in John. Instead, we are told from the very first chapter of this Gospel that Jesus is "the Lamb of God who takes away the sin of the world," and that he will accomplish this glorious task. At the cross Jesus reaches his "hour"—prime time for the redemption of humankind—and is in his element, even forming his new community from the cross in the persons of the Beloved Disciple and Mary. This Gospel is a very different sort of work than Mark or Matthew, but it is no less compelling. To judge from John 20:31 the Gospel of John was written to aid the task of evangelism, not as a tract to be distributed but as a tool for teachers of unbelievers. It is the Gospel where all sorts of people search for Jesus, from John the Baptist to Nicodemus to the blind man to the Greeks to Mary and Martha, and in their seeking he finds them and calls them by name (see the story of Mary Magdalene in John 20). This Gospel writer does not confine himself to short, pithy sayings of Jesus or to short, pithy narratives. Rather, he often offers extended treatments of discourse and narrative. It has been said that this Gospel is shallow enough for a baby to wade in but deep enough for an elephant to drown. The Fourth Gospel is a constant reminder that Jesus was a figure who fit no formula; he was a larger figure than any one portrait could convey. Thus we rejoice there are four Gospels and not just one.

Like the Gospel of Luke, the Fourth Gospel has a universal flavor to it. It was written at a time and in a place where the universal nature of the gospel needs to be underscored (see John 3:16), and salvation is being readily offered to all sorts of people. The tradition that it comes from Ephesus may be true. There is certainly nothing against such an idea; the book of Revelation may support this general locale for the source of all the books associated with "John" (the Gospel of John, the epistles of John and Revelation). The community being addressed has heard portions of the Gospel story before (see John 11:2, which refers to a story not mentioned until John 12). Under the impetus of the death of the Beloved Disciple (see John 21:22-23), the Fourth Evangelist has assembled the man's memoirs and shaped them into a Gospel of the ancient biographical sort.

AND SO?

What have we learned from this thumbnail sketch about the origins of the earliest Gospels? That they indeed were written in the first century A.D., and that all of these documents have some historical interest in Jesus and the movement he spawned, whether they were writing an ancient biography or an ancient historical monograph. We have also learned that there doesn't seem to be any reason to doubt that these Gospels were composed by those who had access to eyewitnesses and the earliest preachers of the good news, as affirmed in Luke 1.1-4. (Mark relied on Peter; the First Evangelist drew on Mark, his own unique material (M) and a special sayings collection of Jesus' words (Q); Luke relied on various eyewitnesses, on Paul, who had contact with Peter, James and John, as well as on Q; the Fourth Gospel was based on the testimony of a Judean eyewitness and the Beloved Disciple.) We see no efforts in these texts or in the ascriptions applied to these texts to cover up their origins. Indeed, they are very frank about their origins. What second-century Christian would make up the notion that Mark and Luke composed two of the seminal Gospels when neither of them were either eyewitnesses or apostles, unless they indeed were the authors?

These Gospels aren't the stuff of which conspiracy theories can reasonably be made. And it needs to be stressed that all four of these Gospels, like Paul's letters and other portions of the New Testament, paint a picture of a Jesus that is both human and divine. It's not even possible to say that the earliest sources on these matters paint Jesus as less than divine, because actually our earliest discussion of Jesus and his life comes in Paul's letters from the 50s, and he presents a very high view of Jesus, as a glance at a text like Philippians 2:5-11 will show.

It's simply not true that the earliest Gospel material portrayed Jesus as merely a man and a prophet. The biblical Gospels are the earliest Gospels, and they portray Jesus in exalted terms, each one in their own way. But if *The Da Vinci Code* is wrong about the original Gospels and their character, then it's also wrong about the beginnings of Christian history and the later handling of these matters in church councils.

HIS STORY, HISTORY
AND THE CANON'S STORY

In *The Da Vinci Code* we find some rather startling claims about Constantine and the formation of the canon (a list of officially recognized and authoritative books). The protagonist of the book suggests that the canon was essentially formed by Constantine and that the books chosen were picked from about eighty Gospels (pp. 231-32). The fact that there weren't eighty Gospels to choose from and that some of those, such as the Gnostic *Gospel of Philip*, are not Gospels at all forces us to ask whether *The Da Vinci Code* really is good history.

In chapter five we will deal with the scholarly attempt to discredit the canon and privilege other later sources of information about Jesus and the Christian movement, but here it is important to present what went on in Christian history, particularly in the discussion about Jesus in the second through the fifth centuries, which led to the great councils and the canonizing of the New Testament. Is it true that there was a great suppression of documents at that juncture? Was a vote on the divinity of Christ really taken, and was it close? Inquiring minds need to know. We will discuss Constantine at the close of this chapter, but first we will consider the development of theological views of Christ as it has a bearing on the development of the New Testament canon.

THE SECOND CENTURY

Without doubt, the theologian who summed up the thought of the second-century church and dominated the intellectual landscape prior to Origen was Irenaeus. He held that the logos (the Word) was God's imminent rationality used in creation, and that the Word coexisted with the Father from all eternity. Irenaeus gave a fuller role to the Spirit and its divine status than others had before, and no doubt this helped foster further trinitarian reflection. It is interesting that Irenaeus identified not Christ but the Spirit as the preexistent Wisdom figure. Thus apparently the Spirit was also preexistent and coeternal with God. Though Irenaeus is closer to trinitarian thinking than anyone before Tertullian, he still did not talk about three coequal persons in a Trinity, but rather a Father with his rationality or wisdom. This was not accidental, however, because Christianity struggled on two fronts—against pagan polytheism (the belief in many gods) and against charges of polytheism from Jews, both of which caused Irenaeus to insist on the belief that God is one. While at points Irenaeus learned from and echoes Justin Martyr, he repudiates the latter's tendency to subordinate the Son to the Father and affirms the true divinity of Christ.

After Irenaeus, the next crucial figure is Tertullian (A.D. 160-220). Tertullian is the first to actually use the word *Trinity*, and perhaps one of the first writers after the New Testament period to insist on the personal preexistence of the Son (see Philippians 2:5-11), though he also argued that the Son was begotten for the work of creation. Tertullian introduced the term *persona* (person) to describe the Word or Son before the incarnation. He held that the three are manifestations of the one divine power. They may be distinguished, but not divided. Father, Son and Spirit are one in substance. He adds, however, that the Father is the whole substance, and the Son is a part of the whole.

In other words, *God* is the name of the substance, the divinity. At some points Tertullian was also willing to say, since the Godhead is one, the Father and the Son are one identical being. This means that monarchianism, or traces of it, was found even among those who were later deemed orthodox on the Trinity. It was apparently not until near the end of Tertullian's life that the standard pattern of trinitarian thinking began to emerge. Nevertheless, Tertullian helped to shape the later councils' discussions, not only on the interrelationships within the Trinity but also on the two natures but single personhood of Christ.

THE THIRD CENTURY

About A.D. 250 Novatian picked up where Tertullian left off and went further, not only saying that the Son was a second preexistent person but insisting that the generation of the Son is not tied to creation but happened before and outside of time. Since the Father is always the Father, there must have also always been a Son. Still we must bear in mind that we do not yet have the three-in-one formula. Novatian still argues that the Father connotes the unique Godhead.

Origen (A.D. 185-254) is one of the most influential figures in this whole discussion. His views were both brilliant and eclectic. He argued that God is a monad (one, not three), but that God always needed to have objects to exercise his goodness and power. So God brought into existence a world of spiritual beings or souls coeternal with him. This idea came to him from Middle Platonism, which spoke of the eternal nature of the world or matter. But, for Origen, the Son was generated before time and the creation of the world to mediate between God and them. The Son is therefore called by Origen a second God. He is willing to state that there are three persons, and each of the three are distinct. Father, Son and Spirit are one in essence but different in subsistence. Sometimes when Origen talks about the oneness issue, it appears that he means the three persons of God are united in a mere moral union. They are said to be one in unanimity, harmony and identity of will. The Father is the fullness of deity, from which the Son and Spirit derive their deity, though these latter two are really and eternally distinct.

There were, however, problems perceived with Origen's use of Middle Platonic notions to help flesh out the understanding of God and the world.

For one thing, maintaining that the world is eternal seems to impugn God's absolute sovereignty and transcendence over the world. It also raises serious questions about what Genesis 1 means when it says God created the heavens the and earth. In addition, Origen sometimes erred when he argued that the Son shouldn't be prayed to because he was an emanation from the Father or even a creature—the first in a chain of emanations (another Platonic idea). This notion was expanded on by the Gnostics in the second and third centuries, who seem to have independently drawn on Platonic and perhaps other Eastern ideas. What is at issue here is whether the divine Son fundamentally belongs to the Godhead or to creation.

THE FOURTH CENTURY

Perhaps most of the West's debate about Christ's divinity that led up to the Council of Nicaea centered around the question of what the Gospel of John means by "the Word became flesh" (John 1:14). Some, like Hippolytus, a student of Irenaeus, had argued that the preexistent Son put flesh on like a human puts on a garment. Tertullian, however, articulated what was to become the standard notion of the two natures of Christ (calling them two *substantiae*, two substances). He said the Son descended into the virgin Mary as a divine spirit and had a real human birth, really assuming human flesh. Foreshadowing issues that were not to be settled until A.D. 451 at Chalcedon (if they can be said to be fully settled even then), Tertullian argued that Jesus' human nature was complete, including a real human soul. This view was later to be disputed by some who wanted to argue that the divine logos took the place of the human soul so the logos dwelled in a human body. This view, however, was seen to deny Christ's true humanity and that he had two complete natures.

Clearly there was a lot of ferment on these issues between A.D. 300 and 450. Some seemed to argue that the divine in Christ should be called "spirit," which sometimes was confused with the Holy Spirit. This view, however, was largely displaced by the idea that *logos* was the term for the divine in Christ. Both Ignatius and Irenaeus simply called the logos the

Son. "Logos" and "Son of God" became the dominant titles in the second and third centuries, and these were used to explain all the main passages in the Gospels and Epistles that were already gathered and being treated as sacred tradition.

Matters were brought to a head by Arius, who argued that (1) the logos was a created being, (2) God wasn't subject to suffering or change, but the logos was, and (3) being subject to change, Jesus was not fully divine. The real issue here was whether God's nature could incorporate change (for example, take on a body), and if this was not so, then apparently Jesus as the logos could not be called God, strictly speaking. For Arius, only God was God, the divinity was a monad, not a triad.

To respond to Arianism the church turned to the word *homoousios* (meaning, "of the *same* substance") and to the phrase "begotten, not made." This amounted to saying Christ came from the essence or very being of the Father. The point at issue was whether or not the preexistent logos was of the same stuff or nature as the Father. If the answer was yes, then he had to be placed on the divine side of the dividing line between God and humans, not on the other side and not somewhere in between. This point was crucial not only for understanding Christ's nature but also our salvation, because if only God could save human beings, then Jesus must be in some sense God (or share in the same divine nature). But some then asked, If we affirm Christ is of the same nature as God, does this mean sharing the same *kind* of nature (made of a similar substance) or sharing the same *identical* nature?

This discussion led some in the early fourth century to argue for a compromise term, *homoiousios* ("of *like* substance"). At Nicaea this compromise term was rejected in favor of *homoousios*, meaning that the Son was of the same, not just a similar or same kind of, substance as the Father. This in turn preserved a union between the Father and Son, avoided two (or even three) gods and still allowed for a distinction between Father and Son as different persons. Father and Son were distinguishable, but not separable. The logic behind the decision at Nicaea appears to have been that since the divine nature is immaterial and indivisible, then any being sharing in the Godhead must share the very same divine substance (essence or nature) as the Father. Thus, in the end the unity of the Godhead and the deity of Christ were affirmed at Nicaea.

This is not to say that there weren't residual concerns. These and other problems were argued about during the entire period between A.D. 325 and 450, and the doctrine of the Trinity wasn't hammered out before that latter date. Until then the arguments over the unity and diversity within the Godhead raged.

One of the more overlooked aspects of the discussion was what to say about the Spirit. It doesn't appear that there was any substantial Christian document written about the deity of the Spirit before the second half of the fourth century, well after the Council of Nicaea. Nicaea had primarily been about the relationship of the Father and the Son. As late as A.D. 380 Gregory of Nazianzus summed up the problem as follows: "Of the wise among ourselves, some have conceived of him [the Holy Spirit] as an activity, some as a creature, some as God; and some have been uncertain what to call him." Clearly, the study of the nature of the Spirit was trailing behind the study of the nature of Christ at this stage of church history.

Two of the key figures who helped resolve the issue were Athanasius (296-373) and Basil the Great of Cappadocia (330-379). They made a start toward sorting out several of these issues by pointing out that (1) the Spirit is called the Spirit of the Lord, hence the Spirit is of God, (2) blaspheming the Holy Spirit is equivalent to blaspheming God, and (3) the Holy Spirit is God because he did what only God could do—make human beings holy, sanctified. Athanasius pointed to the baptismal formula ("in the name of the Father and of the Son and of the Holy Spirit") in Matthew 28:19, and stressed that the church only baptized people into God. This was very helpful, but what was still needed was agreed-on terms for the *oneness* and *threeness* of God. In general the church agreed that in Greek the formula is one *ousia* and three *hypostaseis,* and in Latin one *substantia* with three *personae.* Today we speak of one God in three persons. Apparently it wasn't until

the time of Augustine that the church became really comfortable with talking about three persons in the Godhead.

THE FIFTH CENTURY

What sort of dilemmas led to the Council of Chalcedon in A.D. 451? First,
there was the growing influence, especially in the Eastern church, of Greek
philosophical ideas on theological thinking about God. If God was absolutely impassible (unfeeling) and unchangeable, then God could not suffer. What then should be done with such New Testament phrases as "they
crucified the Lord of glory." How could God be said to die on the cross? If
it wasn't God who died on the cross, how could Christ's death be infinite or
universally effective? Or again, the Fourth Gospel says the Word became
flesh. Did this mean a divine being took on human nature or that the Word
left its divinity behind?

Or was one to think of some sort of amalgam of divine and human natures in Jesus, so that his flesh had become divinized? Another question was
whether some remarks in the Gospels and Epistles applied only to Jesus'
human nature and others only to his divine nature. Thus, it was asked,
when a biblical text says Jesus died and this applied only to his human nature, where did his divine nature go? Why did Christ cry out, "My God, my
God, why have you forsaken me?" (Mark 15:34).

Some pointed out that the Gospel traditions and the Epistles simply referred to Jesus as a person, with *all* the various remarks predicated of him
as a human. In other words, the canonical Gospels didn't make the philosophical and theological distinctions that were later so important. Wouldn't
it be better to say all these statements are predicated of Jesus, the God-man,
as a whole person? For in all such remarks the whole Jesus is the subject or
object of the discussion. It is the *person* who wills and acts and is the object
of actions, not just one nature or other. Unless we separate the two natures
and come up with two Sons (one the human, the other divine), we must say
what happened to one nature also happened to (or at least affected and was
evident to) the other nature. These were the kinds of discussions and co-

nundrums the church pondered, and this is what prompted the Council at Chalcedon.

Cyril of Alexandria (c. 375-444) proved most influential in this discussion. He argued for the helpful notion of the communication of divine and human properties. This posits that the two natures of Christ were so closely united that what might technically be said only of the divine nature of Christ could be said of his human nature as well. Yet there were those who wanted to maintain that Christ had only one nature. Apollinarius (c. 310-390) maintained that only so could Christ be one person. How could we talk about Jesus growing in wisdom and stature if he was omniscient? How could he be like other human beings in all essential respects if he did not experience human limitations of time, space and knowledge? How could he undergo real temptation if it was impossible for him to sin (his divine nature making it impossible)? How could he be fully human if he didn't really have a human spirit?

The problem could be summed up as follows—in Christ the divine and human had to be united closely enough to effect divine salvation for humans, but at the same time not obliterate his true humanity (making his temptations, weaknesses, anxieties and fears a charade). Nor could the union be such that it meant the divine suffered. Strictly speaking, this is impossible if we mean God "feels bodily pain," since God is spirit.

The Council of Chalcedon dealt with these knotty problems in several ways. First, we must not talk about Jesus' natures without setting up a timetable. Are we talking about the preexistent Word before the incarnation, or Jesus Christ during his earthly ministry, or the God-man after the resurrection and ascension? Different remarks were seen to apply to the whole person at different stages of his career. The fathers at Chalcedon were careful not to go to an extreme in interpreting Philippians 2:5-8, that is, they did not argue that Christ gave up his divinity in order to become human. Rather this passage was viewed as the bending down of divine compassion, renouncing divine privilege or status, but not divinity. One and the same Christ was the subject of all predicates relating to him. The final decision at Chalcedon combined the insights of several previous statements by various people. While it did not answer all the questions or solve all the problems, it insured that the church believed in one Christ with two united but distinct natures. In their own words the council declared:

> Following therefore the holy fathers, we confess one and the same Lord Jesus Christ, and we all teach harmoniously that he is the same perfect in Godhead, the same perfect in humanity, truly God and truly human, the same of a reasonable soul and body; the same with the Father in Godhead, and the same with us in humanity, like us in all things except sin; begotten before all ages of the Father in Godhead; the same in the last days for us and for our salvation born of Mary the virgin, the God-bearer, in humanity one and the same Christ, Son, Lord, unique; acknowledged in two natures without confusion, without change, without division, without separation, the difference of the natures being by no means taken away because of the union, but rather the distinctive character of each nature being preserved, and each combining in one person and *hypostasis*—not divided or separated into two persons, but one and the same Son and only-begotten God, *Logos*, Lord Jesus Christ; as the prophets of old and the Lord Jesus Christ himself taught us about him, and the Symbol of the Fathers [the Apostles' Creed] has handed down to us.

I have provided only a small portion of the discussion and debate about Christ from A.D. 100-450. Our focus has been on how the discussions about the Trinity, and especially Christ's role in the Trinity, developed. Obviously, a good deal of the discussion went beyond the New Testament data. The questions of this period raised the issue of which was normative for Christian belief and practice: the sacred traditions (that is, the Bible) or the councils' decisions? And which books were authoritative for the church? Therefore, it is not an accident that during this same period (A.D. 100-451) the church was also sorting out its doctrine of the canon (see the chart "Development of Canon and Christology" on page 62).

Development of Canon and Christology

Development of Canon	*Development of Christology*
(those who affirmed the 27 books of NT)	A.D. 325 Council of Nicaea
	• rejects Arianism
	• promulgates Nicene Creed
	• asserts *homoousios* doctrine
A.D. 367 Athanasius (in the East)	
	A.D. 381 Council of Constantinople
	• rejects Apollinarianism
	• safeguards Christ's humanity
A.D. 382 Synod in Rome Pope Damascus	
A.D. 393 Synod in North Africa A.D. 403 Pope Innocent I [West]	
	A.D. 451 Council of Chalcedon
	• asserts two natures doctrine

What this chart indicates is that there was widespread agreement on what constituted the New Testament canon before the issues related to Jesus' divine nature were all ironed out. The Council of Chalcedon already used an agreed on sacred tradition as the basis for its discussions. This undoubtedly helped the council sort out the theological issues.

While the agendas of the New Testament writers and formulators of the creeds were not always the same, it can't be said that the creeds really *contradict* what the New Testament sources say or suggest, except perhaps in the matter of the impassibility of God. By and large these councils were simply extrapolating what was implied in the New Testament or synthesizing ideas in various New Testament texts. In other words, the fathers were functioning more as systematic theologians than as exegetes.

THE ROLE OF CONSTANTINE

Perhaps the most important point of this discussion is that the canonizing process came to a conclusion *before* the theological issues about Christ were all sorted out. This clearly demonstrates the false accusation that the councils imposed a high view of Christ on the church and so on the canon.

The New Testament documents themselves had, from the first century

A.D., set the agendas that were further developed by the orthodox and re-acted against by the Gnostics. All theologies were not created equal, and all were not equally faithful to the Christ and the earliest witnesses to him. Certainly we ought to be thankful that Gnosticism and other adventurous groups helped to define the boundaries of thought that was consistent with the New Testament. But Gnosticism, as interesting as it is, can't be said to be in accord with or representative of a genuine tradition that can be traced back to Jesus and his earliest witnesses. Indeed, in crucial ways Gnosticism contradicts those witnesses.

What then did the Emperor Constantine have to do with all of this pro-cess? Constantine ruled as Roman Emperor from about A.D. 313 to 337. The truth of the matter is that he didn't take full control of the empire before 324, or very shortly before the Council of Nicaea. This fact alone should make evident that most theological issues, including those about Christ's nature, had taken a rather definite shape and trajectory before Constantine had anything to do with them.

It is open to debate to what degree Constantine himself became a Chris-tian. Certainly, Constantine showed some favoritism toward the Christian faith after it had experienced persecutions under Diocletian and other em-perors, but it is clear that he also continued to honor various pagan gods and customs throughout most of his life, even confirming the privileges of cer-tain pagan priests shortly before he died. He took a pluralistic approach to the empire's religions but was wise enough to see that Christianity had a bright future.

Seeing the rising tide of Christianity, Constantine was astute enough to include it among the approved and even favored religions of his realm. Tak-ing the evidence we have, it simply won't allow us to believe that a person like Constantine would have imposed Christianity on the entire empire. Our interest in Constantine comes chiefly from the fact that he seems to have presided at the Council of Nicaea in A.D. 325, and he also seems to have aided various bishops in two disputes about Christ—Donatism and Arianism. At the Council of Nicaea, Constantine seems to have favored

Christ's true divinity, but he was no theologian, and it certainly wasn't he who wrote the Creed of Nicaea. Nor can it be said that he determined the canon. Constantine mainly pronounced the benediction on the deliberations that had already been formulated.

Is it true, as *The Da Vinci Code* states, that Constantine sought to unify the whole empire under one religious banner (pp. 232-33)? *No*. Is it true, as this novel also states, that Jesus was not affirmed to be Son of God or divine before the Council of Nicaea? *Absolutely not*. Such views of Christ had been held among Christians for the better part of three hundred years before the Council of Nicaea.

Is it true that there was a close vote on the divinity of Christ at Nicaea? The issue at Nicaea was how the divine Son and Father were interrelated and whether they shared the same divine substance. No one at the council was contending that Jesus was a mere mortal or just a prophet, as Teabing asserts in the novel (p. 233). Rather, the dispute was over whether Christ had a divine substance *like* the Father's or whether he shared the *same* divine substance with the Father. The debate was certainly not about whether Christ was divine at all, nor was a vote taken about such a matter. The question was, in what sense was he divine?

It is certainly false to assert, as Brown has through Teabing, that "by officially endorsing Jesus as the Son of God, Constantine turned Jesus into a deity who existed beyond the scope of the human world, an entity whose power was unchallengeable" (p. 233). Constantine simply endorsed what the bishops he was working with had long affirmed and what many Christians had believed for centuries. To see the church's elevated view of Christ as being a result of power politics is a total distortion of the historical evidence. But this is not all.

Teabing also asserts, "Constantine commissioned and financed a new Bible, which omitted those gospels that spoke of Christ's human traits and embellished those gospels that made Him godlike. The earlier gospels were outlawed, gathered up, and burned" (p. 234). Constantine is portrayed in this novel as both kingmaker and canon maker, but in fact neither assertion is true. Constantine supported the various synods, helping them to carry out their decisions. What Eusebius's *Life of Constantine* does say is that the emperor commissioned copies of the Scriptures, which the church had agreed were authoritative and apostolic, to be made and distributed. This is a very different matter than commissioning a new Bible that omitted Gospels that referred to Christ's human traits. And in any case which Gospels does Teabing have in mind? We have already seen how the biblical Gospels depict both the human *and* divine traits of Jesus, which are far different than the Gnostic documents.

Eusebius also says that Constantine took action against some heretics and their secret lore and books—in particular against Novatians, Valentinians, Marcionites, Paulians and those called Cataphrygians. The Valentinians and Marcionites are the most crucial to us, for this means that action was taken against Gnostics and Marcionites, both of whom had basically abandoned the Old Testament, and the latter had whittled down the authoritative Gospels to one, Luke. Eusebius says nothing of "earlier Gospels," and the Gnostic Gospels were neither earlier than the New Testament books nor did they do a better job of revealing Christ's humanity.

CONSPIRACY THEORY?

Everyone likes a good conspiracy theory, especially one that involves power politics and revelations about corrupt institutions. Americans especially love pulling for the underdog, and Brown and the scholars he relies on have very effectively portrayed the Gnostics as underdogs who were discriminated against and didn't get a fair hearing. However, it's not true that the Gnostic documents were suppressed prior to the formation of the canon, nor can it be said they weren't given a fair hearing. They were available for a very long period of time—well over a century. In fact we know that the Gnostic documents were widely copied and read by many Christians in Rome, Asia Minor, Africa and elsewhere. These documents weren't suppressed; they simply weren't recognized as having the same worth or authority as the canonical documents. Once the canon began to crystallize and close, Constantine took some action against the nonauthoritative books, which had long been known and read.

By A.D. 367 Athanasius in the East and various authorities in the West recognized as Scripture only the four canonical Gospels and the twenty-three other documents. In other words they recognized the very same books in our present-day New Testament translations, no more and no less. The evidence of Irenaeus and others, however, shows that this was just the logical outcome of a long process of sifting the relevant documents, particularly documents claiming to be Gospels. We have noted how the four canonical Gospels as well as the letters of Paul were already circulating widely in the second century A.D. and were widely recognized as the truthful Word of God. Constantine did not engineer this canonizing process, though of course his endorsement of Christianity helped this new religion to spread widely thereafter.

The upshot is that the objections raised by *The Da Vinci Code* to the traditional view of Christian history and the canonizing process are false.

PART TWO

Mary Magdalene and the
New Gnosticism

FIVE

SOMETHING ABOUT MARY

At one juncture in *The Da Vinci Code,* Leigh Teabing argues that the church had to suppress the notion that Jesus was married because "a child of Jesus would undermine the crucial notion of Christ's divinity and therefore the Christian Church" (p. 254). What seems to be underlying this contention is the false notion that if Jesus had sexual relationships with a wife and sired offspring, it would be defiling, or perhaps that as a divine being Jesus couldn't afford to be fully human. This of course is not what the creeds suggest: Jesus was fully human and fully divine.

NUPTIAL NONSENSE IN THE DA VINCI CODE

At the outset, there is no reason why Jesus couldn't have been married. Because Jesus was fully human, marriage simply would be an expression of his human nature. Since it isn't the teaching of Jesus that sex was defiling, indeed he speaks of it as the means by which the two become one flesh with each other as God intended (see Mark 10), there is no reason why a married Jesus could not have had sexual relationships and even offspring. Clearly, to judge from texts like Mark 9–10, he loved children. Later ascetic piety (both Christian and Gnostic) had problems with these things, not Jesus. Jesus chose to remain celibate for the sake of bringing the saving reign of God on earth.

In the first part of this book I explained why it is most unlikely that Jesus was married and that there is no evidence that Jesus was married to Mary Magdalene. However, just because Mary was not "the Holy Grail," to use the language of *The Da Vinci Code,* doesn't mean that she wasn't an important figure in the Jesus movement and in Christian history. She certainly was, and in this chapter we will examine what can be legitimately said about Mary Magdalene as a key figure in early Christianity.

Unfortunately, Mary has become a sort of poster child for all sorts of causes, including the new gnosticism, but this misuse of the Mary traditions should not lead us, to slight or belittle her real significance. She was, after all, (1) one of Jesus original traveling disciples in Galilee, (2) present at his death, (3) one of the first, if not the first, to visit Jesus' tomb, (4) the first to see the risen Lord, and (5) the first to testify to the male disciples about the Easter events, in effect becoming the first to preach the Easter message. All of this is worth reflecting on in some detail.

MARY, MARY, EXTRAORDINARY

Over the last few years there have been some extravagant claims made about Mary Magdalene. Was she really Jesus' paramour? Did she become a famous preacher after the Easter events? Did she later found Christian communities with distinctive (feminist or Gnostic) theologies? Just this past month a doctoral thesis came across my desk dealing with the surprising number of medieval stories about Mary Magdalene that have absolutely no basis in the New Testament. This of course doesn't mean all such stories are completely false, but clearly they have to be examined with a critical eye, especially when they seem to have no connections to the traditions that go back as far as the second century A.D. What then can we say with some certainty about Mary Magdalene?

First, her name was surely not Mary. It was Miriam, which is also true for the mother of Jesus. This means she was named after the prophetess of Old Testament fame (see Exodus 15:20-21), and was obviously a Jew. Second, her last name was not "Magdalene." Like many ancient Near Eastern peoples of the era, including Jesus, she was distinguished from other persons of the same name through her place of birth or main residence—in this case Migdal, or as it came to be called Magdala, a very tiny fishing village on the northwest corner of the sea of Galilee, an area we know that Jesus evangelized.

One of the more extraordinary things about Jesus, which seems to have distinguished him from other early Jewish sages, is that he was itinerant and recruited followers. What is even more shocking is that he recruited and traveled with both female and male followers. This would most certainly have been scandalous to most early Jews, who believed that women should travel only with their own kin. But Mary Magdalene was one of Jesus' Galilean disciples and traveled with him and the other disciples.

Mary Magdalene is not mentioned in Mark, the earliest Gospel, before the stories about the last week of Jesus' life; the same is true for second earliest Gospel, Matthew. And in John's Gospel she's not mentioned prior to the crucifixion. This doesn't diminish her importance, for in his Passion narrative Mark also tells us that Mary Magdalene and other women traveled with Jesus in Galilee and cared for his needs. He also reports that she traveled with him on his last journey to Jerusalem (Mark 15:41).

The first real mention we have of Mary Magdalene in the New Testament is found in a brief passage in Luke 8:1-3, but before we examine this passage it is important to make a crucial point. Luke is a careful historical writer, and he doesn't introduce Mary Magdalene into the story until Luke 8:1-3. Had the story about the sinful woman in Luke 7:36-50 been about Mary, Luke surely would have mentioned her name first at Luke 7:36. If he had wanted his first reader, Theophilus, to think that Mary Magdalene was the sinful woman of Luke 7, he would have named her in that narrative. Otherwise, Theophilus would never have thought that the sinful woman was Mary Magdalene. The medieval tradition (first advocated in a sermon by Pope Gregory the Great in A.D. 591) that Mary was a prostitute is false, which ironically is one of the few things *The Da Vinci Code* is right about in its critique of later Christian ideas about Mary. In an age before there were chapters and verses in the text of the Gospels, it's easy to see why the story in Luke 7:36-50 might be confused with the immediately following story in Luke 8:1-3. Nevertheless, it's wrong to associate the two stories as if they are talking about the same woman.

So, Luke 8:1-3 is the first place in this Gospel we hear of Mary

Magdalene, and we are told that she was a follower of Jesus and that Jesus had cast seven demons out of her. Jesus was certainly widely known as and criticized for being an exorcist. What then had happened to Mary Magdalene when Jesus came into her life and helped her? Sometimes modern and even postmodern people have assumed that exorcism texts are simply about people who had mental illnesses or epilepsy. While that is perhaps true in some cases, the fact is that over many centuries there has been credible crosscultural testimony to the reality of evil spirits and the effectiveness of exorcism. The reality is that occult and astrological practices existed in Jesus' day and in every century since, and it is precisely these sorts of practices that have often led to spiritual problems. Mary Magdalene may well have been such a practitioner. She may have dabbled in the occult and believed in the powers of darkness. From her time, for example, we know of curse tablets on which one person would invoke a curse on another, calling on a particular spirit or demon to blight the one mentioned. It's possible that Mary had used such rituals to try to gain some power over whatever misfortunes she was experiencing. Whatever the case was for Mary, Jesus actually was dealing with some spiritual malady in the life of the woman from Magdala.

Notice that Luke 8:1-3 says that Jesus cast seven demons out of Mary. Seven was the number of completion or perfection, and so we are meant to think that she was particularly captivated by the dark presence in her life and required deliverance by an external power or source. Jesus delivered Mary from this condition, and this apparently prompted her to drop everything to follow him around Galilee. We are also told in Luke 8:1-3 that she and other women helped provide for the traveling disciples, which may mean that she was a person of means. We cannot be sure of this, however, because she may have simply cooked or cleaned for others. Joanna, the wife of Chuza, Herod's estate manager, is more clearly a high-status person who may have provided funds for the group of disciples.

Consider, for a moment, the effect it must have had on Galileans that the controversial teacher from Nazareth had both male and female disciples (the latter being unprecedented), and he even traveled from place to place with this entourage. Not only was this unprecedented, it was scandalous. Men and women were supposed to travel with members of their own family. Of course, Jesus claimed his disciples as his brothers and sisters in the faith, but this would not have stopped tongues from wagging. More important, the fact that Jesus both recruited women and allowed them to travel with him on ministry trips tells us that he intentionally took a new and more inclusive approach to women and their roles. Notice too that Jesus does not allow Mary's past association with the demonic to disqualify her from being a traveling disciple.

Then we don't hear of Mary Magdalene again until the Passion narrative. Neither do we know what Mary did during the time between when she first traveled with Jesus in Galilee and this last week of Jesus' life. But Matthew 27:55-56 tells us that several women, including Mary, traveled to Jerusalem with Jesus and the other disciples for the Passover celebration. This tells us at least two things: (1) Jesus associated with and traveled with women and men throughout his ministry, even if this scandalized the more conservative Galileans and Judeans, and (2) it shows just how devoted Mary and others were to Jesus. In their honor-and-shame culture, these women were taking a major risk of becoming outcasts in their own hometowns by traveling and studying with Jesus.

According to Mark 15:40-41 a group of women (Mary Magdalene, Mary the mother of James and Joseph, and Salome) watched the crucifixion from afar, and the first person mentioned in the list is Mary Magdalene. While the male disciples had all denied, deserted or betrayed Jesus, the same could not be said about these female disciples; they were there till the bitter end.

Mark 15:47 says that the two Marys saw that Jesus was buried in Joseph of Arimathea's tomb. Immediately thereafter we have a brief reference (Mark 16:1) to them coming to the tomb on Easter morning. Apparently they were going to anoint Jesus' body and change the linens during the period of mourning. What they found instead was the empty tomb! Mark reports their encounter with an angel at the tomb, always a sign of divine activity, but he doesn't, in the present form of the ending of Mark, tell the story of the appearance of Jesus to these women. (Mark 16:9-20 is missing from all the earliest and best manuscripts of Mark's Gospel.) This same story appears in truncated fashion in Matthew 28:8-10 and in much fuller form in the famous account in John 20, to which we will devote the rest of this chapter.

C. H. Dodd once said that John 20 was the firsthand and most self-authenticating of all the Easter narratives because who would make up the notion that Jesus appeared first to a little-known woman from Magdala? It is a pertinent question. The passage is the story of a soul going from grief to euphoria. But there is much more to the story; it makes apparent that Mary Magdalene, like the other disciples, wasn't anticipating an encounter with the risen Jesus. This came as a total surprise and shock. The resurrection was no dream or wish projection of an overheated imagination but a profound encounter that completely changed Mary's life.

Part of the transformation the Fourth Evangelist stresses is that Mary can no longer cling to the old Jesus, whom she tellingly calls Rabbouni, "my teacher" or "my master." She seems to assume that things will return to the way they were before the crucifixion. Jesus didn't command "touch me not," as some Bible versions have rendered it, but rather "don't cling to me"; that is, don't hold on to the Jesus of the past. Instead she is to go forward, into the future, proclaiming that Jesus is risen and has appeared to her.

This text has generated much of the speculation about Mary's relationship with Jesus, her role in the early church and the like. Why has it had such an impact on later Christian and Gnostic literature? This narrative in John 20 is likely a fuller form of the encounter recorded in Matthew 28. Although Matthew 28 tells us two Marys discovered the empty tomb, apparently the Fourth Evangelist has chosen to focus on the experience of Mary Magdalene, for at John 20:2 Mary says "we don't know where they have put him," which makes it appear she is speaking for the group of women. This is not a small point, because in the Gnostic literature, particularly in the

Gospel of Mary, the risen Jesus uniquely revealed himself to Mary. The Gnostic literature wishes to paint Mary as the exception to the rule that Jesus revealed himself only to men. Mary had somehow, as the Gnostic phrase goes, "made herself male" or at least gender free, and so she received a special revelation. John 20 suggests that her experience was a shared one, even though the Evangelist focuses on the reaction of Mary.

This brings up an important point. The Gnostic literature is written by those who wish to get beyond human sexual matters, who see such material things as hindrances to the core of a person's true identity. Thus it is *not* true that women are more affirmed as women in the Gnostic literature than they are in the canonical Gospels. Quite the opposite is the case. The Gnostic literature is all about transcending or ignoring one's material or bodily identity. But the canonical Gospels affirm maleness and femaleness as a part of the goodness of God's creation. At its heart Gnostic literature has a flawed theology of creation and, not surprisingly, a flawed theology of salvation—salvation is wrongly assumed to be a matter of knowledge that allows a person to transcend the mundane.

Notably, the portrayal of the Easter events involves great restraint on the part of the Evangelist. On the one hand, nowhere is Jesus' resurrection itself actually described. Of course, there were no human witnesses to this event. What is seen is the risen Jesus. On the other hand, when an encounter with Jesus is described at some length, we are told that a woman (or some women) were the first to see the risen Jesus. Both of these factors make perfectly clear that the Evangelist is not "inventing" the story. In a patriarchal culture the author wouldn't make up the notion that women were the first witnesses of the risen Jesus. And in a culture hungry for miracles, he avoids describing the greatest miracle of all—the resurrection of Jesus. These factors attest to the integrity of this narrative. Notice too that the Gospel narratives don't indulge in pure apologetics here. Jesus appears to his own disciples, not to the skeptical or to strangers. The resurrection is seen as an event that brings to full flower the faith of those who had already been disciples. The Gospel narrative focuses on the impact of the risen Jesus on the community of his followers.

From John 20:11 on we note a gradual progression of revelation to Mary, which she doesn't get until the crucial moment of recognition and the even more crucial teaching that follows it. Compare Mary (verses 11-12) to Peter (verse 5). Mary's activity at the empty tomb is similar to Peter's, only Mary is apparently more spiritually perceptive than Peter because she sees angels in the tomb, and Peter doesn't. Angels here, as elsewhere, signal that divine activity is in progress — they are involved in the absence of Jesus' body from the tomb. These angels seem to send the implicit message not only that Jesus is no longer present in the tomb but that Mary should look elsewhere. In short, she should stop dwelling on the Jesus of the past.

The near silence of the angels in this account contrasts somewhat with the accounts in Mark 16:1-8 and its parallels in the Synoptics. In John 20:13 the angels ask a question that sets in motion a dialogue with Jesus. They inquire: "Woman, why are you weeping?" Notice that neither the empty tomb nor the presence of angels is sufficient to bring Mary out of her sorrow and grief. The Evangelist wishes us to think that nothing less than the presence of the risen Jesus could transform her spiritual outlook. In this respect she is similar to Thomas (John 20:25), but in actuality there is a world of difference. Thomas continues to be unbelieving even though his closest friends and fellow disciples claim to have seen the risen Lord. Mary may be forgiven for her obtuseness, for no one had seen the risen Jesus before she did. Mary's problem is that she is fixated on the past, and it is no accident that in this highly charged, symbolic narrative, only after Mary turns *away* from the empty tomb does she actually see Jesus.

At John 20:15 Jesus reiterates to Mary the question of the angels: "Woman, why are you weeping?" However, it is only when Jesus calls her by name (see John 10:3-4 on the shepherd calling the sheep by name) that Mary recognizes him. Jesus is approaching Mary as the good shepherd, gently leading her away from her preoccupation with death and the past. Yet her mental horizons are still fixed on the past, for she responds to his voice with "Rabbouni." She has yet to see or acknowledge him as the risen Lord.

Notice also that Jesus asked, "*Whom* are you looking for?" He is hinting that she should be looking for a person, not a corpse (a "what"). At first she thinks Jesus is the gardener and asks where Jesus' body has been laid. In the Gnostic literature Mary is depicted as much more enlightened than others who encounter Jesus beyond his death. But in the biblical Gospels, Mary's initial lack of spiritual perceptivity could hardly be clearer. Ironically, her master, the one whom she has listened to so often before, speaks to her and she mistakes him for the gardener! (Yet we shouldn't be too hard on Mary, for Jesus isn't immediately recognized by others either. For example, see the Emmaus road story in Luke 24:13-35.)

This is so very different from the Gnostic text that proclaims Jesus loved Mary more than others precisely because her understanding and perceptiveness was so much greater. This brings to light another problem with the Gnostic literature. It views the divine-human encounter as "deep calling to deep," not as pure grace. In Gnostic literature, salvation is a self-help program for those who are capable of responding to insider knowledge.

It becomes clear at verse 16 that it is no longer adequate to relate to Jesus as a teacher or great sage. Now he must be seen as more than just a conveyor of wisdom. Mary must progress to a new stage in her understanding of Jesus. When Mary grasped Jesus, his response was "Stop clinging to me," not, as I noted earlier, "Don't touch me." Mary is approaching Jesus with a view to the past, and Jesus puts a stop to it. Had modern speculators such as Dan Brown recognized the nuance of this narrative, they would not have made the mistake of assuming that this confirms that Mary had a physically intimate relationship with Jesus. Notice the contrast between the way Jesus commands Thomas to touch him (John 20:27) and the way he rebukes Mary here. Jesus doesn't want Mary to embrace him. This is hardly a family reunion scene between husband and wife! In fact, Jesus isn't interested in renewing relationships with Mary or anyone else on the old terms, for he is no longer the old Jesus. He is now truly on the way to returning to the Father. In a little while he would no longer be with the disciples in the flesh, so he doesn't want Mary to depend on a temporary state of affairs.

Throughout the Fourth Gospel, one of the keys to understanding who Jesus is, is to know where he has come from and where he is going, that is, from and to the heavenly Father (see John 7:33; 13:3; 14:12, 28; 16:28). Similarly, Jesus' disciples come to full understanding of themselves and their roles only when they understand where their commission comes from and where they are being told to go. The key to understanding Jesus comes not from knowing where he was at the moment but where he was going—he would be lifted up in glory as he returned to the Father. If we understand this, then we have a good grasp of Jesus. Until Jesus ascends, the disciples can't have equal access to him. Until Mary grasps this, rather than grasping Jesus, her own pilgrimage can't come to completion. Having learned where Jesus is going, she gets the point and bears witness to the male disciples. Significantly, Jesus, who speaks about his "brothers" needing to be told (verse 17), reestablishes his relationship with them through a "sister," Mary. John 20:18 says emphatically—"Mary Magdalene went and announced to the disciples, 'I have seen the Lord.'" These words demonstrate that Mary is no longer fixated on the past but rather focuses on the task before her. It was enough that Jesus had spoken to her about a spiritual relationship in the present tense, one that would continue beyond his ascension. Mary becomes an example of the disciple who doesn't need to see or touch and yet believes (see John 20:29).

It is no accident that in this resurrection narrative the Fourth Evangelist spends so much time on this encounter between Mary and Jesus. She was last at the cross, first at the tomb and first to see and proclaim the risen Lord. In other words, Mary became *the* witness to the heart of what later was to become the creed. It is a grave injustice to this story to separate Mary from these experiences and depict her as an early Gnostic who received a special revelation from Jesus on the basis of her perceptiveness or inner light.

Clearly, Mary's focus in this story is on the historical Jesus, and she above all proclaims the truth that Gnostics didn't want to affirm—Jesus came back from death in the flesh, having died on the cross for human sins.

There could hardly be a more emphatic rejection of Gnostic theology (the inherent evil of matter, including the human body). Mary should not be co-opted as a witness to a message that doesn't focus on the death and resurrection of Jesus. This is a travesty, one that Mary, if she were present to speak for herself, would surely repudiate. She was a good Jew, looking for the promise of resurrection and restoration of God's people, and she encountered it in Jesus.

Here we have a very clear endorsement that it is all right for women to proclaim the gospel. After all, if Jesus could commission a woman to do this, who are we to object to such things? Here we have an honestly told tale that neither hides Mary's spiritual obtuseness at the beginning of the story nor her bold witness to the male disciples at the end of the story. It is neither a surprise nor inappropriate that the third-century church father Hippolytus called Mary the "apostle to the apostles."

Even today, sadly, parts of the church haven't fully grasped the implications of this story for the ministerial roles of men and women called and commissioned by God. But this sin and oversight by the church shouldn't cause anyone to turn to Gnostic Gospels in hopes of finding a better paradigm for women in ministry. For those who hope to find an adequate theology of human sexuality, the goodness of creation or the full equality of men and women in Christ, the sign over the door of Nag Hammadi reads: "Abandon hope, all ye who enter here."

The New Testament tells us nothing more of Mary, nor does any other first-century Christian literature, such as the *Didache*. She disappears into the sands of time, and the later conjectures about her seem to have little or no historical basis. But a strong case can be made that she was an important early disciple of and witness to Jesus, and we can say with equal certainty that there is absolutely no early historical evidence that Mary's relationship with Jesus was anything other than that of a disciple close to her Master.

THOSE IN THE KNOW

I n a particularly egregious example of the historical errors that pockmark *The Da Vinci Code*, the scholar and Grail enthusiast Leigh Teabing argues:

> Fortunately for historians . . . some of the gospels that Constantine attempted to eradicate managed to survive. The Dead Sea Scrolls were found in the 1950s hidden in a cave near Qumran in the Judean desert. And, of course, the Coptic Scrolls in 1945 at Nag Hammadi. *In addition to telling the true Grail story, these documents speak of Christ's ministry in very human terms.* . . . The scrolls highlight glaring historical discrepancies and fabrications, clearly confirming that the modern Bible was compiled and edited by men who possessed a political agenda—to promote the divinity of the man Jesus Christ and use His influence to solidify their own power base. (p. 234, emphasis added)

We are also informed that the earliest Christian records are the Dead Sea Scrolls and the Nag Hammadi documents (p. 245).

Were it not for the enormous impact of this novel, I might be tempted to laugh and shrug off such historical mistakes. As any scholar who has studied the Dead Sea Scrolls will tell you, there isn't anything Christian about them. They are the documents and library of early Jews who lived at the Dead Sea. No Christian documents have been found there. The Dead Sea Scrolls don't "speak of Christ's ministry" at all. Teabing should surely know better.

But what of the Nag Hammadi scrolls? Should these documents be called Christian? Do they present the true historical Jesus, showing that the New Testament is part of an attempt to elevate a mere teacher and prophet to divine status? Do they really present us with a more human Jesus? These questions deserve close investigation.

While the Nag Hammadi documents draw on New Testament characters, episodes and ideas, they are neither a direct critique of the New Testament nor an exposé of its discrepancies. However, most of these Gnostic documents are permeated with a philosophy and theology that is at odds with fundamental tenets of the Judeo-Christian tradition, tenents grounded in the Hebrew Scriptures and the Greek New Testament.

Though it may be fashionable to include the Gnostic texts along with the New Testament as equally valid sources of the truth, *both* can't be correct about the historical Jesus or the movement he set in motion. I quite agree that the Nag Hammadi documents deserve a close and fair reading. The same historical-critical scrutiny should be applied to them as to the Scriptures. But those who undertake such a scholarly enterprise quickly find that the Gnostic documents rarely take them back to the historical Jesus. And in the places where the Gnostic documents disagree with the biblical material, they prove to be less authentic witnesses than the New Testament.

BACK TO THE DESERT OF EGYPT

The Nag Hammadi documents, found in a storage jar by two brothers digging in the soil in 1945, are currently housed in the Coptic Museum in Cairo. When the brothers first took these documents home, their mother used some of the papyrus to stoke the fire of her bread oven! The rest were rescued and eventually made their way to the museum. Though these once-secret documents were hidden from the public eye in a storage jar, they are now available to anyone who has the time and patience to study them. Indeed, since they all have been translated into English, we can read them without benefit of learning Coptic or Greek or any other ancient language. Elaine Pagels's *The Gnostic Gospels* has become a popular resource about the Gnostic texts we are most concerned with, but in fact she doesn't present us with the texts but merely analyzes them at some length. The Nag Hammadi library, as it is best called, includes a wide array of differing kinds of documents. We must be cautious about judging documents that are part of a library. I would hardly want someone to judge my own theology on the basis of some of the books currently found in the Asbury Seminary library, where I teach. Nevertheless, close scrutiny of the Nag Hammadi library is very revealing.

Consider, first, the contents of the thirteen codices (or books) that contain these Nag Hammadi documents. Look at the table of contents on the next page. What immediately jumps out is that not a single Old or New Testament book is included! If the community that owned these documents had the Bible as we know it, this library doesn't show it. However, it's plausible that these works were deliberately hidden from view, perhaps in the fourth or fifth centuries when certain works deemed heretical were ferreted out and done away with.

Several factors indicate that these documents did not come out of a distinctive church community but rather out of an isolated monastery in the Egyptian desert:

- First, these documents were found at the base of a mountain where there is also evidence of a Byzantine-period grave area. One of the caves in the grave area has an inscription in Coptic with lines from the Psalms. These documents seem to have come from one of several nearby Christian monasteries where a certain amount of speculation and open philosophical discussion was permitted. Scholars have suggested that the Nag Hammadi documents were buried several miles away from a Christian monastery because they had come under suspicion. In other words, we do *not* have clear evidence from these documents that a separate Gnostic community existed.

- Second, the carton that came with codex VII also contained fragments of a biblical codex, a homily and a letter from Pachomius, perhaps the monk for whom the nearby Basilica of St. Pachomius is

Nag Hammadi Library Table of Contents

Codex I
1 *The Prayer of the Apostle Paul* (colophon)
2 *The Apocryphon of James*
3 *The Gospel of Truth*
4 *The Treatise on the Resurrection*
5 *The Tripartite Tractate*

Codex II
1 *The Apocryphon of John*
2 *The Gospel of Thomas*
3 *The Gospel of Philip*
4 *The Hypostasis of the Archons*
5 *On the Origin of the World*
6 *The Exegesis on the Soul*
7 *The Book of Thomas the Contender*
  (colophon)

Codex III
1 *The Apocryphon of John*
2 *The Gospel of the Egyptians*
3 *Eugnostos the Blessed*
4 *The Sophia of Jesus Christ*
5 *The Dialogue of the Savior*

Codex IV
1 *The Apocryphon of John*
2 *The Gospel of the Egyptians*

Codex V
1 *Eugnostos the Blessed*
2 *The Apocalypse of Paul*
3 *The (First) Apocalypse of James*
4 *The (Second) Apocalypse of James*
5 *The Apocalypse of Adam*

Codex VI
1 *The Acts of Peter and the Twelve Apostles*
2 *The Thunder: Perfect Mind*
3 *Authoritative Teaching*

4 *The Concept of Our Great Power*
5 *The Republic* 588b-589b
6 *The Discourse on the Eighth and Ninth*
7 *The Prayer of Thanksgiving* (scribal note)
8 *Asclepius* 21-29

Codex VII
1 *The Paraphrase of Shem*
2 *The Second Treatise of the Great Seth*
3 *The Apocalypse of Peter*
4 *The Teachings of Silvanus* (colophon)
5 *The Three Steles of Seth* (colophon)

Codex VIII
1 *Zostrianos* (cryptogram)
2 *The Letter of Peter to Philip*

Codex IX
1 *Melchizedek*
2 *The Thought of Norea*
3 *The Testimony of Truth*

Codex X
1 *Marsanes*

Codex XI
1 *The Interpretation of Knowledge*
2 *A Valentinian Exposition*
3 *Allogenes*
4 *Hypsiphrone*

Codex XII
1 *The Sentences of Sextus*
2 *The Gospel of Truth*
3 *Fragments*

Codex XIII
1 *Trimorphic Protennoia*
2 *On the Origin of the World*

named. This may confirm the theory that the Nag Hammadi library came from a nearby monastery.

- Third, the colophons and some scribal notes in the manuscripts show they were studied by pious Christians—Christian prayers are inscribed in several of the codices (I, II and VII). Most book copying in the early Middle Ages took place in monasteries, and the monks frequently would copy all sorts of documents without necessarily endorsing all the documents' contents. We also know that in response to a letter from Athanasius, Pachomius's successor, Theodore, purged heretical books from his monastery in A.D. 367. Possibly the Nag Hammadi documents were hastily buried by monks who objected to their destruction, but this is just a conjecture. It has been suggested that these Nag Hammadi documents were not in use for very long, because there is material in codex VII that shows it was produced after A.D. 348. Furthermore, the lid of the jar in which these codices were placed dates to the fourth or fifth century A.D. This means that they were used no more than 150 years and probably less.

Every one of the fifty-two Nag Hammadi documents appear to be Coptic translations of Greek documents, which suggests that they are translations from an earlier period, perhaps some of them even going back to the second century A.D. We can say this with some assurance in regard to the *Gospel of Thomas* because earlier Greek fragments of this document have also been found.

One of the more crucial conclusions that has resulted from several decades of scholarly study of the Nag Hammadi texts is that they are not a "library" from a single sect or religious group of people. Some of these documents deserve to be called Gnostic and some don't. What does unite these documents—and this important conclusion counts against the impression we are left with by *The Da Vinci Code*—is that almost all these documents reflect asceticism. This seems to be why they were gathered together. They provided some support and guidance for the ascetical lifestyle of monks.

Most of these texts, however, are also Gnostic in their theological and philosophical character.

Some of these documents subscribe to a particular brand of Gnosticism and a particular mythological system associated with it, namely, that Adam's son Seth was the spiritual father of a gnostic race of Sethians. Seth is also portrayed as a revealer figure in this literature. While none of the Gnostic documents we are mainly concerned with reflect this line of thought, these Sethian documents do show two relevant things about Gnosticism: (1) it could be highly speculative in character, and (2) it focused more on philosophical ideas than on historical events or persons. This isn't a surprise since Gnosticism doesn't value mundane events, processes or persons.

The most famous school of Gnosticism is the Valentinian school. One of the Nag Hammadi documents is directly attributed to the Gnostic Valentinus (*A Valentinian Exposition*). But several more come from his strain of Gnosticism: the *Prayer of Paul*, the *Gospel of Truth* and, most importantly for our purposes, the *Gospel of Philip*. It is probable that the *Gospel of Mary* comes from this strain of Gnosticism as well, though the *Gospel of Mary* is not part of the Nag Hammadi collection. (It first came to light in 1896 in Cairo.) Valentinus, certainly one of the most prominent names associated with Gnosticism, began as an orthodox monk in the second century A.D. After he lost an election to be a bishop, he went in a Gnostic direction, which his contemporary Tertullian called a lapse into heresy. His real influence in terms of Gnosticism came in the last third of the second century. (Remember, there is no evidence that Gnosticism existed before the second half of the second century.) So there was perhaps a couple of centuries of development before Gnosticism was officially repudiated, but it is clear enough from Tertullian and Irenaeus that it was already deemed heretical by major figures in the second century.

It's difficult to appreciate how very different in character the Gnostic Gospels are from the canonical Gospels without actually reading them. To give you a better feel for them, I have provided a few representative samples.

THE GOSPEL OF PHILIP AND THE GOSPEL OF MARY

Like other Gnostic documents these Gospels see self-knowledge as the essence of salvation, and indeed even appear to urge the worship of human beings. The *Gospel of Philip*, for example, says at one juncture "God created [man and] man created God. So it is in the world. Men make gods and they worship their creations. It would be fitting for gods to worship men." Thus, Gnostics seek the divine element within themselves.

Showing how very different the Gnosticism of the *Gospel of Philip* is from the claims of the canonical Gospels is not difficult. Consider for example the following quotation from the *Gospel of Philip*:

Some said, "Mary conceived by the holy spirit." They are in error. They do not know what they are saying. When did a woman ever conceive by a woman? Mary is the virgin whom no power defiled. She is a great anathema to the Hebrews, who are the apostles and [the] apostolic men. This virgin whom no power defiled [. . .] the powers defile themselves. And the lord [would] not have said "My [father who is in heaven]" (Mt 16:17), unless [he] had had another father, but he would have said simply "[My father]."

This passage has a variety of problems. Notice, for instance, that the Holy Spirit is identified as a woman. It also highlights another factor that permeates Gnostic documents, namely, they have an anti-Semitic quality. Being a Hebrew, or Jewish, is not good. This text also reflects knowledge of what the canonical Gospels claim ("My [father who is in heaven]"), and its author is not afraid to contradict it in various important ways. For example, in regard to the resurrection of Jesus we hear:

Those who say that the Lord died first and (then) rose up are in error, for he rose up first and (then) died. If one does not first attain the resurrection he will not die. As God lives, he would [. . .].

This not only affirms the preexistence of Christ but also of other humans. Resurrection in the flesh then is redefined as human conception leading to physical birth. Consider this further passage from the *Gospel of Philip*:

> Some are afraid lest they rise naked. Because of this they wish to rise
> in the flesh, and [they] do not know that it is those who wear the [flesh]
> who are naked. [It is] those who [. . .] to unclothe themselves who are
> not naked. "Flesh [and blood shall] not inherit the kingdom [of God]"
> (1 Co 15:50). What is this which will not inherit? This which is on us.
> But what is this, too, which will inherit? It is that which belongs to
> Jesus and his blood. Because of this he said, "He who shall not eat my
> flesh and drink my blood has not life in him" (Jn 6:53). What is it? His
> flesh is the word, and his blood is the holy spirit. He who has received
> these has food and he has drink and clothing.

Notice that this passage includes a quote from Paul and from the Gospel of
John. There are also quotations from Matthew's Gospel and from the Gnostic *Gospel of Thomas*. Clearly this document is written later than the New
Testament. More telling for our purposes is the following quote, which refers to Mary Magdalene:

> For it is by a kiss that the perfect conceive and give birth. For this reason
> we also kiss one another. We receive conception from the grace which
> is in one another.
>
> There were three who always walked with the lord: Mary his mother
> and her sister and Magdalene, the one who was called his companion.
> His sister and his mother and his companion were each a Mary.

This passage is followed by another, which we have dealt with in part earlier
in this book.

> As for the Wisdom who is called "the barren," she is the mother [of
> the] angels. And the companion of the [. . .] Mary Magdalene. [. . .
> loved] her more than [all] the disciples, and used to kiss her [often]
> on her [. . .]. The rest of [the disciples . . .]. They said to him, "Why
> do you love her more than all of us?" The savior answered and said to
> them, "Why do I not love you like her? When a blind man and one

who sees are both together in darkness, they are no different from one
another. When the light comes, then he who sees will see the light,
and he who is blind will remain in darkness."

This Gospel is named after Philip because of the following passage:

> Philip the apostle said, "Joseph the carpenter planted a garden be-
> cause he needed wood for his trade. It was he who made the cross
> from the trees which he planted. His own offspring hung on that
> which he planted. His offspring was Jesus and the planting was the
> cross." But the tree of life is in the middle of the garden. However, it
> is from the olive tree that we get the chrism, and from the chrism, the
> resurrection.

As in Gnostic teaching generally, any flaws that exist in creation, including
humans, are blamed on some malignant deity, perhaps the so-called Demiurge, which is a lesser god who made the tainted material world. This lesser
god is charged with making a grave mistake, as follows:

> The world came about through a mistake. For he who created it
> wanted to create it imperishable and immortal. He fell short of attain-
> ing his desire. For the world never was imperishable, nor, for that
> matter, was he who made the world. For things are not imperishable,
> but sons are. Nothing will be able to receive imperishability if it does
> not first become a son. But he who has not the ability to receive, how
> much more will he be unable to give?

Not only so, but since creation is fallen from the outset, then normal ways
of relating, such as marriage and intercourse, are seen as inherently defiling.

> No [one can] know when [the husband] and the wife have inter-
> course with one another except the two of them. Indeed marriage in
> the world is a mystery for those who have taken a wife. If there is a
> hidden quality to the marriage of defilement, how much more is the

undefiled marriage a true mystery! It is not fleshly but pure. It belongs not to desire but to the will. It belongs not to the darkness or the night but to the day and the light. If a marriage is open to the public, it has become prostitution, and the bride plays the harlot not only when she is impregnated by another man but even if she slips out of her bedroom and is seen.

Salvation, according to Gnostic thinking, is a matter of knowing the right things, which don't include the death and resurrection of Jesus Christ.

He who has knowledge of the truth is a free man, but the free man does not sin, for "he who sins is the slave of sin" (Jn 8:34). Truth is the mother, knowledge the father. Those who think that sinning does not apply to them are called "free" by the world. "Knowledge" of the truth merely "makes such people arrogant," which is what the words, "it makes them free" mean. It even gives them a sense of superiority over the whole world. But "Love builds up" (1 Co 8:1). In fact, he who is really free through knowledge is a slave because of love for those who have not yet been able to attain to the freedom of knowledge. Knowledge makes them capable of becoming free.

Before I comment on any of these texts in more detail, I will first present some material from the *Gospel of Mary* as well. The *Gospel of Mary* has been more difficult to piece together because there is a Coptic version and two different Greek versions, and the text is in poor condition. Another problem is that the Coptic and Greek versions don't match up. At any rate, in the *Anchor Bible Dictionary* Pheme Perkins suggests that this Gospel (as well as the *Gospel of Philip*) was composed toward the end of the second century A.D. This date is arrived at because the Greek papyrus of this Gospel is from early in the third century, and the *Gospel* itself was likely composed not long before. Once again there is absolutely no historical evidence that this text and its special interests has its origins in the first century A.D. It is rather the product of the Gnostic movement that arose in the second century.

Like some other Gnostic texts, such as the *Apocryphon of John* and *Sophia of Jesus Christ*, the *Gospel of Mary* presents the risen Jesus as instructing the disciples in the esoteric and secret Gnostic teachings. Like so much of this literature, the *Gospel of Mary* rejects the goodness of the material realm. All matter is subject to passion, disease, decay, death and evil. Gnostics, though, are spiritual, and so they are not to participate in physical passions. The male disciples are commissioned to spread this Gnostic version of the good news, but they despair because of their fear of suffering. Mary Magdalene, however, shames them, reminding them of God's grace and protection. They already have the true Gnostic identity because "he has prepared us and made us into men," a phrase that seems to go back to saying 114 of the *Gospel of Thomas*. (The *Gospel of Philip* defines it as "putting on the perfect man.") Notice that Mary says she too has been made into a man.

Mary is asked by Peter to recount the vision or revelation she has received. This section of the *Gospel of Mary* is mutilated and so we don't have it all. But what we do have teaches about the mind, an intermediary between the soul and spirit, receiving Gnostic revelation. It also tells us how the soul ascends past the cosmic powers on its way to heaven, the place of rest. Hence Mary has insight into the destiny of the soul enlightened by Gnostic wisdom. When Peter objects to this teaching, Levi rebukes him. There is a similar defense of Mary's revelation in the *Gospel of Philip*.

What are we to make of this material? Should we see such texts as an indirect testimony to women teachers in Gnostic circles? This is possible. Should we see Peter as representing orthodox Christianity's objection to such Gnostic revelations? Perhaps so. But what this text doesn't suggest is that Peter objected to Mary having some kind of revelation. The issue here is the substance of her teaching. In other words, I think it's doubtful that these texts attest to the banning of women teachers within orthodox Christianity. In the first place, these documents are from a time when we have clear testimony to women playing prominent roles in early Christianity, including being exemplary martyrs. The famous story of the martyrdom of Perpetua comes to mind. These events and their recounting are from about the same time that these Gnostic documents were written.

Of course it is true that there was opposition to women assuming teaching and preaching roles (both inside and outside the orthodox churches) during and after the second century A.D. In the story of Paul and Thecla (from the second century), Thecla must in essence renounce her female identity and commit herself to absolute chastity to do ministry, but *the same thing can be said of the women discussed in these Gnostic documents.* Not only are these Gnostic books unlikely sources for the theory that Mary Magdalene was married, they are not really very useful sources for some modern feminist agendas. They don't attest to the equality of women and men in Gnostic circles. In the Gnostic texts, women must become "perfect men" to be accepted, and this entails renouncing their physical identity. In other words Gnostics were no less patriarchal in the way they thought about perfection than non-Gnostics. They went even further in that they don't affirm the goodness of any created or fleshly identity!

Karen King seems to suggest that Mary Magdalene is being identified with Wisdom in the *Gospel of Philip,* and so King thinks Mary is the mother of angels and the spiritual sister of Jesus, and indeed his female counterpart. The problems with this analysis are manifold. Wisdom in the canonical Gospels is something Jesus is said to embody, and in Proverbs 8–9 Wisdom is a personified attribute of God. In the *Gospel of Philip,* Mary Magdalene, though she is clearly said to be privy to a special revelation from God, is not touted as the female deity named Sophia (Wisdom). Instead, Mary puts the male disciples to shame. Being shamed, the males then evangelize like good male apostles were supposed to. Mary is used as a shaming device, perhaps to exhort male Gnostics to get on with the Great Commission, only in this case the good news is about Gnostic Wisdom that's only for the few. In the end, Gnostic literature is no friend to Christian women. Better to turn to the New Testament itself, which does affirm a variety of roles for women, including teaching and prophesying (see Acts 18 or 1 Corinthians 11).

WHY THE NEW GNOSTICISM?

But why have the more radical feminist scholars gravitated toward the Gnostic literature if it is not all that helpful in supporting some of their agendas? In a moment of candor Elaine Pagels tells us that her study of the Gnostic literature has helped her "clarify what I cannot love: the tendency to identify Christianity with a single, authorized set of beliefs—however these actually vary from church to church—coupled with the conviction that Christian belief alone offers access to God."

Now it must be said that this remark is both amazing and highly ironic. The authors of the Gnostic documents are often more dogmatic than any of the orthodox Christians! They insist that people must have the Gnostic wisdom or their souls will not ascend to heaven. They aren't early advocates of religious pluralism or feminism, and they shouldn't be made the poster children for such a modern crusade.

Clearly both Christians and Gnostics were offering mutually exclusive truth claims, and both thought they offered the one way to salvation and the true knowledge of God, *and they were right about the issue of mutual exclusivity.* Both of these belief systems can't be true if the law of noncontradiction holds any water. Either one or the other is truly Christian, but not both. And according to our earliest sources, the New Testament documents, Christianity affirms the goodness of creation, the incarnation of Christ, the death and bodily resurrection of Jesus, salvation by grace through faith in the atoning death of Jesus, and the public proclamation of the gospel to all. Faith and salvation are more a matter of Who you trust than how much you know. Gnosticism affirms none of these.

Instead of listening to Elaine Pagels or Karen King about this complex and confusing Gnostic literature, we would do better to listen to the Orthodox journalist Frederica Mathewes-Green.

The problem wasn't the insistence that we can directly experience God. It was that Gnostics' schemes of how to do this were so *wacky*. Preposterous stories about creation, angels, demons, and spiritual hierarchies multiplied like mushrooms. . . . The version attributed to Valentinus, the best-known Gnostic, is typical. Valentinus supposedly taught a hierarchy of spiritual beings called "aeons." One of the lowest aeons, Sophia, fell and gave birth to the Demiurge, the God of the Hebrew Scriptures. This evil Demiurge created the visible world, which was a bad thing, because now we pure spirits are all tangled up in fleshy bodies. Christ was an aeon who took possession of the body of the human Jesus, and came to free us from the prison of materiality.

"Us," by the way, didn't mean everybody. Not all people have a divine spark within, just intellectuals; "gnosis," by definition, concerns what you *know*. Some few who are able to grasp these insights could be initiated into deeper mysteries. Ordinary Christians, who lacked sufficient brainpower, could only attain the Demiurge's middle realm. Everyone else was doomed. Under Gnosticism, there was no hope of salvation for most of the human race.

This is hardly literature that comforts the marginalized or the oppressed. To the contrary it is elitist to the core. Gnostic literature is intellectually arrogant.

In addition, at various points Gnostic literature is blatantly anti-Semitic. Like Marcion, Gnostics sometimes repudiate both the Hebrew God and the Hebrew Scriptures. But what is deeply offensive to Jews and Christians is the notion that salvation is a self-help program, an exercise in which one pursues self-knowledge and self-awareness. Gnosticism also repudiates God's work in history, making esoteric knowledge what matters.

It is orthodox Christianity that affirms life and matter. As Eugene Peterson so aptly puts it:

Matter is real. Flesh is good. Without firm rooting in creation, religion is always drifting off into some kind of pious sentimentalism or sophisticated intellectualism. The task of salvation is not to refine us into pure spirits so that we will not be cumbered with this too solid flesh. We are not angels, nor are we to become angels. The Word did not become a good idea, or a numinous feeling, or a moral aspiration; the Word became flesh. It also becomes flesh. Our Lord left a command to remember and receive him in bread and wine, in acts of eating and drinking. Things matter. The physical is holy. It is extremely significant that in the opening sentences of the Bible, God speaks a world of energy and matter into being: light, moon, stars, earth, vegetation, animals, man, woman (not love and virtue, faith and salvation, hope and judgment, though they will come soon enough). Apart from creation, covenant has no structure, no context, no rootage in reality.

In light of the evidence it is certainly puzzling why scholars like Elaine Pagels, Karen King and others are so enamored with Gnosticism. They aren't ascetics—they have yet to withdraw from the world and deny the goodness of matter in general and bodies in particular. Frankly, the ancient Gnostics would have repudiated these scholars. In fact, they would have seen these scholars' revisions of Christian history on Gnosticism's behalf as an unnecessary enterprise since focusing on real events in space and time isn't worthy of a truly spiritual person.

Perhaps these scholars have been burned in one way or another by orthodox Christianity. Thus they are looking for an alternative path of quasi-Christian redemption that will justify their rejection of basic New Testament truths. It's almost as if they said to themselves, "If the first-century documents don't suit my belief system, I'll find some other early materials and rewrite the history of the first century." In other words it seems that these scholars are creating a new myth of Christian origins, one that better suits their own more human-centered approaches to religion. Of course, this is only conjecture, but at least it makes some sense of why scholars would so strongly embrace literature that is not agreeable to some of their personal values. This is a sad and tragic form of grasping at straws, because there are no viable alternatives other than rejecting the whole of early Christianity and its history.

DOUBTING THOMAS

Funny thing about Thomas: he has become the patron saint of those who have honest doubts about Jesus—or of those who have questions that need to be answered or of those who seek a personal experience of Jesus to overcome their doubts. This is ironic because what Jesus actually says about Thomas isn't that he had doubts but that he was "unbelieving" *(apistos;* John 20:27). Unbelief is not commendable in the biblical Gospels. What does this have to do with the Gnostic *Gospel of Thomas?* Very simply, in the *Gospel of Thomas* the risen Christ revealed himself to Thomas in a direct way, and therefore Gnostics speculate about what secret wisdom the post-Easter Jesus imparted to him.

Without question the most celebrated of all the Gnostic or semi-Gnostic documents is the *Gospel of Thomas,* or more properly speaking, the *Gospel of Didymus Judas Thomas.* The name *Didymus* means twin (see John 20:24; 21:2). But the twin of whom? Are we being told that Thomas was the twin brother of Jesus, or perhaps of some other member of the inner circle of the disciples? It's not clear in the *Gospel of Thomas,* but this Thomas seems to be the same as the one mentioned in the Gospel of John.

For a few years now some scholars have argued that the *Gospel of Thomas* is the real key to understanding Jesus' teachings, the inside scoop that penetrates back before the time of the biblical Gospels. Analogies have been drawn between the *Gospel of Thomas* and Q, the collection of Jesus sayings that both Matthew and Luke apparently used in composing their Gospels. Q, like *Thomas,* was mostly a collection of Jesus' "greatest hits"—by which I mean his most famous sayings.

WHAT IS A GOSPEL?

Some scholars have suggested that there was an early form of Christianity that didn't focus on the Passion and resurrection of Jesus. Instead it concentrated on the teachings of Jesus. The *Gospel of Thomas* has been offered as proof that there was such a group of Christians, for clearly this document doesn't recount those events. But is it fair to call the *Gospel of Thomas* a Gospel, anymore than Q can be called a Gospel? There are two problems with such a designation.

First, the term *gospel* ("good news") is not just a Christian term, but rather one that was already in use in the Greco-Roman world before the canonical Gospels were written. Because the ancient world didn't have a free-market economy, public gifts from higher-status persons were what greased the wheels of society and commerce. Emperors were lauded for their good deeds of benefaction and their triumphs in wars. The "gospel" was good news about actions taken on behalf of the people by the emperor (or another wealthy person). The benefactors weren't, in the main, praised for their great philosophical or wise utterances.

When early Christians picked up the term *gospel*, they had in mind the good news of things Jesus had done, while also including some of his teachings. For example, the earliest Gospel, Mark, is mostly action—focusing on Jesus deeds. It is doubtful that the earliest Christians would have seen a mere collection of teachings, without a recounting of Jesus' saving activities, as a Gospel. Q might be a part of a Gospel, as it is in Matthew and Luke, but it is not a Gospel on its own. On this account it's doubtful that we should see the *Gospel of Thomas*, mostly a collection of teachings, as a Gospel. But there is another reason to doubt that Thomas represents the earliest form of a Gospel.

By common consent among a wide range of New Testament scholars, of the New Testament Gospels Mark's Gospel is the earliest, followed by Matthew, Luke and John. If you examine this material closely, Gnostic literature most closely resembles the Gospel of John because John contains extensive discourses and dialogue. The next Gospel that the Gnostic literature most resembles is Matthew, because Matthew has more than five blocks of teaching material. What this tells us is that the later the Gospel, the more likely it was to include more teaching materials, and it is no accident that the two biblical Gospels most often cited in Gnostic literature are John and Matthew, precisely because they more often contain Jesus' teachings.

If we take a moment to examine the sermon summaries in Acts (see, for example, chaps. 2 and 13) or turn to our earliest New Testament documents, the letters of Paul (see, for example, Philippians 2:5-11), we discover that the earliest preaching about Jesus focuses on his *activities* and who he is. I sometimes like to ask my students, "Could we be saved if Jesus never told the parable of the good Samaritan?" Immediately, they say yes, we could. I keep going through one teaching of Jesus after another, and they keep saying yes. I then ask, "Could we be saved if Jesus wasn't the Savior, and if he hadn't come to die on the cross and rise again?" All of them emphatically say no. The most crucial thing is that Jesus came as the Redeemer and died and rose again. Both the earliest preachers and the earliest Gospels, which are the biblical Gospels, agree that for something to truly be good news, it has to include things that Jesus *accomplished* for others, particularly his death and resurrection.

On these terms neither the *Gospel of Thomas* nor the *Gospel of Philip* nor the *Gospel of Mary* deserve to be called Gospels at all. Knowing Jesus' teachings isn't enough to effect salvation. We must believe on him and what he *accomplished* for our salvation. His teaching is important, especially for faithful discipleship, but it isn't the most important thing. This is probably why we find so little of Jesus' teachings in our earliest New Testament documents, Paul's letters, which make up about a third of the New Testament. It is Christ's *deeds* and their significance more than Christ's precise words that Paul preaches. This is worth pondering when wading through the Gnostic Gospels.

One more preliminary consideration is important. I sometimes lecture on the historical Jesus with another New Testament scholar, Professor A. J.

Levine from Vanderbilt. We sometimes start our discussion with three major premises: (1) a non-Jewish Jesus is a nonstarter, (2) so is a Jesus who doesn't look to God's future final activity in the world, and (3) a Jesus who didn't have some sort of Jewish messianic self-understanding is also unlikely. What is striking to me about the Jesus that shows up in the Gnostic literature is that he fails to pass any of these tests. There is no real discussion of the Son of Man (Daniel 7) in this literature, yet Jesus is called other things in these Gospels. The *Gospel of Thomas* even denigrates Jewish rituals such as circumcision. Any sense that Jesus presented himself as a messianic figure for Jews is missing in this literature as is consideration of end times in general. As a historian I am immediately suspicious of the Gnostic Jesus when so much that characterizes him in the biblical Gospels is absent.

A THOMAS SAMPLER

Early on, the *Gospel of Thomas* warns us what is to come. In saying 13 Matthew tells us that Jesus is a "wise philosopher." Part of his philosophy is that the truly important aspect of the enlightened person is the preexistent soul (not the body). Thus in saying 84 Jesus says, "When you see your likeness [in a mirror], you are pleased. But when you see your images that came into being before you and that neither die nor become visible, how much you will have to bear!" And in saying 19 Jesus serves up a conundrum—"Blessed is the one who came into being before coming into being." Thus the enlightened person should discover the divinity within by looking back, not to the future. But the New Testament has a definite orientation toward the future and final redemption. The *Gospel of Thomas* and other Gnostic literature characteristically sublimate or eliminate this eschatological orientation of the teaching of Jesus and replace it with speculation about other worlds, layers of aeons, preexistent souls and the like.

Saying 22 of the *Gospel of Thomas* also reveals how different this literature is from the teaching of Jesus we find in the biblical Gospels:

Jesus said to them, "When you make the two into one, and when you make the inner like the outer and the outer like the inner, and the upper like the lower, and when you make male and female into a single one, so that the male will not be male nor the female be female . . . then you will enter [the kingdom]."

This saying is at odds with the biblical Gospels in two ways. First, this text is probably based on the notion of the androgynous Adam. In Gnostic thought gendered bodily existence is not a good thing, so maleness and femaleness must be overcome. The reuniting of male and female into one person returns Gnostics to that ideal androgynous condition. This is very different from what we find in Mark 10. Here gendered existence is seen as God's original intent, and the union of the sexes doesn't obliterate gender differences but rather allows for their full expression, that is, two committed persons of the opposite gender participate in and share a one-flesh union that is blessed by God, yet they remain male and female.

Saying 18 typifies the Gnostic avoidance of eschatology:

The disciples said to Jesus, "Tell us about the end." Jesus said, "Have you already found the beginning, then, that you seek for the end? For where the beginning is the end will be. Blessed is the one who stands at the beginning: that one will know the end and will not taste death."

Gnostic material is so cryptic that we are never quite sure what the writer is driving at. In this saying we seem to find the idea not merely that the end will be like the beginning (a return to the Garden) but rather that those who know they have come from light (and thus have light within them) already have eternal life. It's not a matter of being saved by grace through faith or faithfully awaiting the full salvation at the resurrection. No, the Gnostic already has eternal life from the beginning.

This view is also expressed more clearly in saying 24: "There is light within a person of light, and it lights up the whole world. If it does not shine, it is dark." As Pagels herself points out, this is very different from what we find in the Gospel of John, where Jesus is the light of the world. Christology (the study of Christ) becomes mere anthropology (the study of humans) in the *Gospel of Thomas*. This becomes strikingly clear in saying 108: "Jesus said, 'Whoever drinks from my mouth will become like me; I myself shall become that person, and the mysteries will be revealed to him.'"

Much of the *Gospel of Thomas* is anti-Semitic. For example, saying 52 begins with his disciples commenting to Jesus, " 'Twenty-four prophets have spoken in Israel, and they all spoke of you.' He [Jesus] said to them, 'You have disregarded the living one who is in your presence and have spoken of the dead.'" Notice that what matters is not what was predicted by the prophets or that Jesus comes from the Jewish royal line, but that he is living quite apart from his physical and ethnic identity. Similarly, in saying 53 Jesus repudiates the Jewish practice of circumcision. If it were beneficial, says Jesus, men would come into the world already circumcised.

The salvation offered in the *Gospel of Thomas* is clearly at odds with the salvation (by grace through faith) offered in the New Testament. For example, in saying 62 Jesus says, "I disclose my mysteries to those [who are worthy] of [my] mysteries." The good news of Christ's salvation is not freely offered to all. A person has to be worthy to receive Jesus' secret wisdom.

Saying 85 avers that Adam is not worthy to be a Gnostic. If he had been worthy, he would not have tasted death. A good deal of Gnostic literature suggests that the elect aren't actually a part of Adam's fallen race, instead they are of a different origin. Sometimes Gnostic literature claims the enlightened ones are of the race of Seth. However, for other Gnostic literature the inner self—the real, eternal image within the outer, fallen shell—is what matters. Physical descent from Adam or Seth is irrelevant. Only the preexistent, spiritual self is important.

This brief sample is sufficient to show that the *Gospel of Thomas* material is different from and at odds with the biblical Gospels. Jesus is presented as the wise philosopher who dialogues with his disciples and helps them see the inner light that is already within them.

THE STRANGE PILGRIMAGE OF THE GOSPEL OF THOMAS

The complexity of the source and interpretation of the *Gospel of Thomas* is sometimes overlooked. Most of this Gospel is only available in Coptic, which appears to be both a translation and an editing of an earlier Greek source. We simply don't have the earliest form of most of the *Gospel of Thomas*, and thus sweeping claims about an earlier Greek form are not demonstrable. Most scholars believe the Greek form of the text is closer to the original *Thomas*. Its origin seem to lie in eastern Syria, where there were various traditions and legends about the apostle Thomas. Most scholars think the original document was written in the second century by someone who admired Thomas, not by the apostle Thomas himself. Be that as it may, it seems likely that the earlier *Gospel of Thomas* was edited in a more Gnostic direction when it was translated into Coptic and was placed in the Nag Hammadi collection.

Of the ancient *Gospel of Thomas* manuscripts we actually have, the Coptic text dates to the middle of the fourth century A.D. and the earliest Greek text dates to about A.D. 200. This makes the earliest physical evidence of the *Gospel of Thomas* considerably later than the Q material we find in Matthew and Luke. The *Gospel of Thomas* includes some twenty allusions to Jesus' teaching in James, and in each case they seem closest to Matthew's form of Q. The difference of the *Thomas* material from both Q and James is precisely why the vast majority of New Testament scholars don't think the Gnostic Gospel gives us the earliest form of the teachings of Jesus in most cases. But even if the *Gospel of Thomas* is from late in the first century, it is the only sayings collection, whether from earliest Christianity or early Judaism, that manifests a Gnostic bent. The *Gospel of Thomas* has more kinship with *Pistis Sophia*, a second-century Gnostic document, than it does with the material in the biblical Gospels or James. Even Philo, who drank deeply from the well of Platonism, is still so biblically oriented and so grounded in the Hebrew Scriptures' creation theology that he would have found some of the notions in the Gnostic material abhorrent.

Besides the many ways the *Gospel of Thomas* differs with the Q material

and the biblical Gospels, in my view two observations are decisive in dating
Thomas later than the material we find in the biblical Gospels. First, as has
been amply shown by Klyne Snodgrass and C. M. Tuckett, *Thomas* manifests a knowledge of not only the material found in all four Gospels, but it
also manifests *the editorial work of all four Gospel writers and especially that
of the Fourth Evangelist.* Second, Thomas reflects knowledge of the editorial work in both M and L, and *this is true even of the Greek version of
Thomas.* As Craig Evans says, this seriously undermines the theory of either
the antiquity or the independence of *Thomas* when compared with the
Gospels of the New Testament. In fact, *Thomas* has very little that is fresh
to offer Jesus research.

If the writer of *Thomas* knows both the unique L and M material, then
he must be writing after those Gospels appeared in the last twenty years of
the first century. But there is more. The *Gospel of Thomas* in some respects
is something of a compendium or anthology of earlier sayings material from
the biblical Gospels, taken mostly verbatim from them. For example, the
following passages compare very closely: (1) Matthew 5:14b and *Thomas* 32,
(2) Matthew 23:13 and *Thomas* 39, (3) Luke 6:45 and *Thomas* 45b, (4) Luke
5:33 and *Thomas* 104a; (5) Luke 5:33-35 and *Thomas* 104b.

Other comparisons are less certain than these, but these are enough to
show that the author clearly knows the canonical Gospels' sayings material.
But this is not all. The *Gospel of Thomas* also reflects knowledge of and al-
ludes to many of Paul's letters, including Romans, 1-2 Corinthians, Galatians, Ephesians, Colossians, 1 Thessalonians, 1 Timothy and other portions
of the New Testament such as Hebrews, 1 John and Revelation. How is this
even remotely possible before the second century A.D.? It's not really possible unless one argues for an even earlier version of *Thomas*, for which there
is no evidence. We could much more plausibly argue that the *Gospel of
Thomas* is a second-century attempt to interpret all sorts of New Testament
ideas and passages in a Gnostic manner. James D. G Dunn draws this conclusion: "The more obvious interpretation of the Nag Hammadi documents is that they are all typically syncretistic: they draw bits and pieces

from a wide range of religious influences in the ancient world, including Judaism and Christianity, but including others too. As such they are totally explainable in terms of what we now know about second- and third-century Gnosticism."

The evidence as we have it means that the *Gospel of Thomas* is a document that at the very least postdates the biblical Gospels and probably also the book of Revelation, which is why I say *Thomas* likely comes from the second century A.D. Of course it's true that *Thomas* depends not only on the materials we have in the biblical Gospels but also on some other materials that are very different in kind. The very beginning of the document prepares us for what we are in for: "Jesus said, Let one who seeks not stop seeking until he finds. When he finds, he will be troubled. When he is troubled, he will be astonished and will rule over all." The expression "all" or "the all" is found regularly in other Gnostic documents in the Nag Hammadi library. This nonbiblical catch phrase "the all," which is often a tip-off that we are dealing with a Gnostic text, points toward the whole of material reality and its influence, passion and beings.

To be fair, a few sayings found in the *Gospel of Thomas* may be derived from oral traditions that may go back to the historical Jesus but are not found in the New Testament. It may even be that *Thomas* sometimes gives us an earlier version of a Jesus saying. However, before we get too excited about a Gnostic Gospel revealing to us a new and more historical Jesus, even the skeptical Jesus Seminar didn't think there was more than a handful of authentic Jesus sayings in the *Gospel of Thomas* that aren't also found in the biblical Gospels. Grandiose claims about *Thomas* and the historical Jesus are definitely unwarranted.

WERE THE EARLY GNOSTICS FEMINISTS BEFORE THEIR TIME?

The *Gospel of Thomas* lends no credence to the notion that the Gnostics were feminists before their time. Consider for example saying 114 in Thomas: "Simon Peter said to [the disciples], 'Make Mary leave us, for females are not worthy of life.' Jesus said, 'Look I shall guide her to make her male, so that she too may become a living spirit resembling you males. For every female who makes herself male will enter the Kingdom of Heaven.'" Even so, the evidence suggests there were women teachers in Gnostic circles, but there were also women teachers among the orthodox Christians. The difference is that in Gnosticism a woman had to renounce her womanhood to have such roles.

So, is it really possible to edit and refashion Gnosticism to make it palatable today? Has Pagels made Gnosticism not merely accessible and understandable but even believable? I think the answer to this question is no. Not even Gnosticism Lite ("less filling, tastes great") can accomplish such an aim for modern women. Hear again the critique of Frederica Mathewes-Green:

> Now you can begin to see what the early Christians found heretical.
> Gnosticism rejected the body and saw it as a prison for the soul;
> Christianity insisted that . . . even the human body can be a vessel of
> holiness, a "temple of the Holy Spirit." Gnosticism rejected the He-
> brew Scriptures and portrayed the God of the Jews as an evil spirit;
> Christianity looked on Judaism as a mother. Gnosticism was elitist;
> Christianity was egalitarian, preferring "neither Jew nor Greek, male
> nor female, slave nor free." Finally, Gnosticism was just too compli-
> cated. Christianity maintained the simple invitation of the One who
> said, "Let the little children come unto me. . . ." Full-blown science-
> fiction Gnosticism died under its own weight.

Pagels does not endorse this aspect of Gnosticism. But the Gnostics would not endorse her version either. They did not think of these elaborate schemes as mythopoeic (which is how Neo-Gnostics describe them), but as factual. Your salvation depended on getting it right, and Gnostics argued with each other much as theologians do today. Some claimed that the body was so evil you had to give up sex; others said the body was so illusory that it didn't matter what you did with it. A well-meaning post-modernist who murmured "You're both right" would be reviled for not grasping what's at stake.

This best-selling book [Pagels's *Beyond Belief*], and its accompanying train of reviews and author profiles, presents a familiar cast of characters. The Gnostics, developers of a variety of Christ-flavored spiritualities in the earliest centuries of the Christian era, are enthroned as noble seekers of enlightenment. The early Church, which rejected these theologies, is assigned its usual role of oppressor, afflicting believers with rigid Creeds. It's the old story of oppressive bad guys and rebellious good guys, and Americans never tire of it. . . .

Early Christians rejected Gnosticism, all right. But what Pagels presents is not the part they rejected.

Gnostic material can be dressed up in ever so eloquent prose, but it still has nowhere to go. Historian Philip Jenkins points out that the scholarly community is aware of the agendas of scholars like Elaine Pagels and Karen King, particularly the agenda to rewrite the history of early Christianity so more options become available for religious moderns who are disenchanted with orthodox Christianity. He says that because of their ignorance of the facts, the general public is quite susceptible to the suggestion of conspiracy theories, misuse of power and the myth of concealment and recent disclosure.

These modern "disclosers," like Pagels or King or even Brown, are like the Gnostic Jesus—providing insider wisdom, or the "real story," that allows those who are uncomfortable with the canon and the orthodox church to find a place in the story. Philip Jenkins puts it this way: "Much modern writing on the hidden gospels and their authors is utterly partisan, with well-defined heroes and villains who are represented quite as starkly and stereotypically as the white-robed saints of motion picture notoriety." Jenkins goes on to add: "Diligent exploration of the very large literature of New Testament scholarship over the last century or so might suggest that the 'new' insight is nothing of the kind, however conveniently the work of past generations will be overlooked. As we have seen, a kind of historical amnesia is a necessary feature of the whole myth of concealment and discovery." Brace yourself; we get to see this Gnostic melodrama actually played out on the big screen when *The Da Vinci Code* shows up in the theaters in the next year or so.

WHAT'S WRONG WITH THIS PICTURE?

At the end of *The Gnostic Gospels* Elaine Pagels wistfully ponders what would have happened if Gnosticism hadn't been suppressed by orthodox Christianity. She thinks that Christianity would not have survived antiquity if it had "remained multiform." In other words, orthodoxy was the theology of the winners, and their power politics enabled traditional Christianity to survive.

Before we subscribe to this vision of things, which mostly misses the point that long before the creeds the books of the New Testament witness to what we call today orthodox Christianity, we should note the word *multiform*. There can be no doubt there was some diversity in early Christianity. Certainly there were arguments and differences in the fledgling Christian movement. We only need to read James and compare it to Galatians, for example. But how much diversity? By *multiform* Pagels isn't referring to the sort of diversity that actually exists within the canon. What Pagels means is that *from the beginning* there were *both* Gnostic and orthodox Christians and so there were radically different visions of the faith coexisting until the power politics of the councils took over (that is, in the fourth and fifth centuries A.D.).

This is a false vision of early Christian history if by "early Christian" we mean the New Testament period itself. We have seen that there are very good reasons to believe that even the *Gospel of Thomas* came from early in the second century at best. In fact it reflects a knowledge of more of the New Testament than even important second-century figures such as Ignatius, Tertullian or Irenaeus! This is indeed strange if *Thomas* was written by somebody who lived at the same time or earlier than these figures.

If the *Gospel of Thomas* is not from the New Testament era, then there is no reason whatsoever to see the Gnostic movement as part of the diversity of first-century Christianity. The *Gospel of Thomas* is certainly not a "fifth"

Gospel that should have been included in the canon. In fact it doesn't have the necessary content to warrant being called a Gospel. It adds precious little to our knowledge of the historical Jesus and nothing of theological significance about Jesus that we didn't already know.

The Gnostic quest for self-knowledge and self-discovery has something of a modern ring to it, but such a quest and the quest for the historical Jesus are very different, and only one of them is authentically Christian. In *Beyond Belief* Pagels openly admits important differences:

> John's message contrasts with that of Thomas. Thomas's Jesus directs each disciple to discover the light within ("within a person of light there is light"); but John's Jesus declares instead that "I am the light of the world" and that "whoever does not come to me walks in darkness." In Thomas, Jesus reveals to the disciples that "you are from the kingdom, and to it you shall return" and teaches them to say for themselves that "we come from the light"; but John's Jesus speaks as the only one who comes "from above" and so has rightful priority over everyone else: *"You are from below; I am from above. . . . The one who comes from above is above all."*

The historical Jesus and the early Christian movement suggests that if we follow Jesus and seek the face of the God who is wholly Other, we will find ourselves. Those who lose their life in the love and wonder and praise of the real God will find it again. But if we seek the god within, we not only will not find ourselves, we will not find God either. God doesn't live at the end of the dead-end street known as the human ego. The fallen self doesn't need to be found or coddled even if it masquerades as the inner light. Our ego needs to be crucified in order that we may become a new creature in Christ, and that requires a relationship with Someone outside of and other than ourselves.

The "final" authority of human experiences (we have all heard the cry "I can't deny my own experience") ring out loud and clear in the Gnostic literature. But unfortunately, genuine human experience is not all good or self-validating. Experience needs to be evaluated on the basis of some valid external criteria, otherwise there is no objective way to tell the difference between a heart-warming experience and heartburn. Both are genuine experiences, but they should be evaluated very differently.

In the earliest days of aviation, during the first two decades of the twentieth century, when propellers had been perfected, pilots encountered a new problem. Now able to fly not only as high as the clouds but directly into them, they found when they did that all of their instincts, and indeed their inner ears, kept screaming at them—"you are diving down to the left, pull up." When they pulled up, the nose of the plane would then point straight up in the sky and the engine would stall out, often resulting in a crash. They had been level all along even in the cloud, but their inner ear and instincts had betrayed them. Their own experience had lied to them.

This problem was finally corrected by adding to the instrument panel a level indicator for the nose of the plane as well as an indicator of when the wings and flaps were level to the ground. The pilot in a cloud could not tell these things by relying on his own inner experience, because air pressure had changed the sense of things in the inner ear.

Gnostic experience was like entering into a cloud of unknowing. One lost one's bearings and one could not see the truth because human experience, rather than the revealed truth in the genuine Scriptures, was seen as the ultimate test of what was real, saving, life-giving, true. In an affective age such as ours it is understandable why one might be drawn to the Gnostic approach to truth, but in the end it amounts to a religious form of flying without the proper instruments (the instruction manual called the Bible). Only the real revelation of God in the Scriptures prevents crash landings.

I was stuck in the airport in Manchester, New Hampshire, not long ago, and I ran the story I have just told by one of the pilots who was also awaiting a lane. He confirmed to me that the story is absolutely true. He added, "The very first lesson on the first day of flying school is 'keep your eyes on the instruments when flying in a cloud and do not look up into the cloud or trust your own inner experience.'" It is good advice when it comes to discerning what is the earliest and truest form of Christianity as well.

PART THREE

Did the Canon Misfire?

CONSULTING THE CANON PROFESSORS

For some time certain scholarly circles have disdained the notion of an authoritative canon of Scripture. This idea is said to be offensive because it privileges certain documents over others. Sometimes this complaint takes the form of urging that we consider all the evidence in all the documents, a perfectly legitimate complaint. But sometimes it arises out of a distaste for the notion of exclusivity—the idea that the twenty-seven books of the New Testament tell the truth and have the truth, and one need not look elsewhere for salvation.

REVISIONIST HISTORY REVISITED

I have already addressed the relationship between the development of the canon of the New Testament and the development of the two natures (fully divine and fully human) of Christ. The most important observation that came out of this is that it's untrue to say that the divinity of Christ was imposed on the church as a result of the councils of the fourth and fifth centuries. To the contrary, the discussions on the natures of Christ were still going on at length well after the twenty-seven book canon was agreed on in both the Eastern and Western parts of the church. In this chapter we will consider some other equally serious claims about the canon.

In *The Gnostic Gospels* Elaine Pagels complains about the canon:

We now begin to see that what we call Christianity—and what we identify as Christian tradition—actually represents only a small selection of specific sources, chosen from among dozens of others. Who made that selection, and for what reasons? Why were these other writings excluded and banned as "heresy"? What made them so dangerous? Now, for the first time, we have the opportunity to find out about the earliest Christian heresy; for the first time, the heretics can speak for themselves.

Pagels goes on to complain that while it's true that the Gnostic texts were rejected because of theological and philosophical differences from the orthodox texts, it wasn't until this period of councils that "orthodoxy" as opposed to "heresy" was defined. She also avers that Christianity as an orthodox, institutional religion didn't really exist prior to the political and social maneuvering of these councils. Politics and religion are what defined "orthodoxy." But is this really true? Was there Rome Pope Damascus no such thing as orthodoxy before the fourth-century councils? Is it true that Gnosticism was harshly suppressed without having a fair trial? Is Gnosticism really the first Christian heresy? The image we get from Pagels is that a bunch of old fourth-century men, institutional church functionaries to the core, went through a pile of papyri and voted on what was in and what was out. Is this really how it happened?

In fact, this revisioning of things is not even remotely close to being true. In the first place, the claim that there is evidence that from the beginning of the Christian movement there were Gnostic Christians alongside orthodox Christians is simply false. Even the *Gospel of Thomas*, probably the earliest Gnostic document, seems to have come from a period *after* the books comprising the New Testament had been recognized as authoritative and widely circulated. Indeed, *Thomas* draws on most of these documents, adding some new ideas to them about Jesus and about the faith. In other words, historians have no business talking about a Gnostic form of Christianity before about the middle of the second century A.D. There is simply no good evidence to support such a claim.

In the second place, Gnosticism wasn't the first unorthodox belief system on the block. It appears likely that the Marcionite heresy precedes it. But even if Gnosticism was first, church fathers like Irenaeus and Tertullian had already labeled it a heresy *in the second century*. Thus it's absolutely false to say that the councils of the fourth and fifth centuries defined *heresy* for the first time and that only then was Gnosticism regarded as heretical.

Yet another falsehood that revisionist historians espouse is that there was no core belief system in first-century Christianity that could later be called "orthodoxy." This is a very strange claim because already in the epistles of John there were discussions about orthodoxy and heresy. Even in Paul's letters we see quite clearly that distinctions are made between truth and error, and by the time of the Pastoral Epistles there is a very clear sense of what amounts to faithful and unfaithful teaching about Jesus and the faith, particularly in the areas of Christ and his salvation.

Furthermore, there is a clear sense of the authoritative and inspired nature of the Old Testament, as 2 Timothy 3:16 shows. This is important because if the Pauline churches and others (notice the use of the Old Testament in the Johannine corpus, in Hebrews and in Luke-Acts) already had recognized the Hebrew Scriptures as canon, a set of authoritative and divinely inspired texts, *we are already at a watershed moment in the development of early Christianity—it could not and would not recognize Gnosticism as a legitimate development of the Christian faith.* Gnostics, we have seen, can't abide a theology of the goodness of creation, which is an essential part of the Jewish Scriptures. I can't stress this strongly enough. Gnosticism was a nonstarter from the outset because it rejected the very book the earliest Christians recognized as authoritative—the Old Testament! (Remember, there was no canon of the New Testament in the New Testament era.) After recounting how very little the Old Testament is referred to in the Gnostic literature, Pheme Perkins comes to the following conclusion:

> Gnostic exegetes were only interested in elaborating their mythic and
> theological speculations concerning the origins of the universe, not

in appropriating a received canonical tradition. They may have even concurred with Celsus's judgment that most of the Old Testament contains historical and legal materials which do not provide keys to a deeper wisdom. [By contrast] The Christian Bible originates in a hermeneutical framing of Jewish scriptures so that they retain their canonical authority and yet serve as witnesses to the Christ-centered experience of salvation. Gnostic and Valentinian exegesis adapts hermeneutics of esotericism to enlist parts of the emerging Christian Bible and the oral traditions about the words of the Savior to frame a different experience of self, world, and salvation.

She has put her finger on one of the main reasons Gnostic texts could never have been included in the New Testament—they largely rejected the Scriptures the earliest Christians affirmed.

During this same time the apostolic and authoritative texts of the New Testament period were being collected. We see this quite clearly in 2 Peter 3:16, which says of Paul: "He writes the same way in all his letters, speaking in them of these matters. His letters contain some things that are hard to understand, which ignorant and unstable people distort, as they do the other Scriptures" (NIV). Even if, as some New Testament scholars think, this text was written in the earliest years of the second century rather than in the first century, it makes perfectly clear that already a collection of Paul's letters were considered authoritative for the church and were put on par with "other Scriptures." The key Greek word in this passage is *graphas* ("Scriptures"), which could be translated "writings," but it is clear enough that the author is not talking about just any kind of writings. He is talking about texts deemed to be Scripture and consulted regularly by Christian people. In other words, the canonizing process had already been set in motion in the New Testament period, and there already was a core of documents and ideas by which other documents could be evaluated. The New Testament documents already were a standard by which truth and error could be distinguished. The creeds simply spelled out the implications of what is already present in those earliest Christian documents and in the discussions of the second through fourth centuries.

That there was a canonizing process well under way in the second century A.D. is clear enough from the existence of the Muratorian Canon list, which includes the biblical Gospels and no others. Furthermore, it was never a question of excluding Gnostic documents that were previously deemed authoritative in the early church. To the contrary, these documents never were included in any of the early canon lists, not even by the unorthodox Marcion (around A.D. 140). In fact, what the second century reveals is that when the Gospel of John, one of the authoritative and widely accepted Gospels, was seen to be favored by the Gnostics, some orthodox Christians even began questioning it.

In other words there was never a time when a wide selection of texts, including Gnostic texts, were deemed acceptable. To the contrary, there was even a time when some of the books that did make it into the New Testament canon were considered suspect—or possibly guilty by association with fringe folks—including the Gospel of John and Revelation. The idea that the early church in the first and second centuries didn't exercise critical judgment when it came to authoritative texts is simply untrue. Indeed, they were in danger of even excluding some books well grounded in the apostolic tradition. Unorthodox documents like the Gnostic texts simply heightened the sense of urgency and probably accelerated the process of recognizing which documents were authoritative.

Thus when the councils, beginning at Nicaea in A.D. 325, discussed such matters, it was the culmination of a long process of reflection on which books were apostolic in character and which were not. Constantine didn't impose orthodoxy on the church. The Council of Nicaea merely formalized what the church in various regions of the empire had been affirming for some time. The Gnostic documents, which had been allowed to circulate for over a hundred years, were tried and found wanting. There never was a time when any known Christian church recognized them as legitimate representations of the orthodox Christian faith. The church correctly concluded that Gnostic documents offered up various forms of false philosophy and esoteric teachings. The New Testament documents written in the first century are the proper litmus test for what counts as orthodoxy.

Of course, Karen King is right when she says that the earliest period of Christianity was a time of grappling with issues. This is perfectly clear from reading Galatians, the earliest New Testament document. She is, however, quite wrong in denying that there was a core set of beliefs shared by all followers of Jesus. Listen to why she thinks the Nag Hammadi library is so crucial to writing a revision of the history of early Christianity:

> These writings are of inestimable importance in drawing aside the curtain of later perspectives behind which Christian beginnings lie, and exposing the vitality and diversity of early Christian life and reflection. They demonstrate that reading the story of Christian origins backwards through the lenses of canon and creed has given an account of the formation of only one kind of Christianity, and even that only partially. The fuller picture lets us see more clearly how the later Christianity of the New Testament and the Nicene Creed arose out of many different possibilities through experimentation, compromise, and very often conflict.

Did you catch the sleight of hand in this analysis? Forget altogether the fourth and fifth century councils and the formation of the creeds. The essential question is, What were the earliest documents (and what do they say)? The answer is the New Testament itself. We have no documents earlier than these, and as any good historian knows, the documents closest to the source of a movement are likely to be most revealing about its origins.

The documents written by eyewitnesses or those in contact with eyewitnesses are our primary sources, and these documents happen to be in the New Testament, plus a few other likely first-century documents, such as the *Didache* and *1 Clement*. There is no good evidence that Gnosticism was one of the dueling forms of Christianity in the first century A.D. Thus the degree of diversity that King thinks existed in the earliest churches is not historically demonstrable. There is no evidence of Gnostics or Marcionites in the first-century churches.

In King's view the earliest Christians modeled wide diversity, and we are called to "emulate their struggles to make Christianity in our own day." So the agenda is laid bare: it's our job not merely to rewrite the history of ancient Christianity but to remake modern Christianity. This clarion call needs to be seen for what it is. It's not simply a rejection of the canonizing process and creedal orthodoxy but also of the limits of first-century Christian diversity in favor of a much broader and more pluralistic model. King calls us to reject our earliest historical sources, the New Testament, as the basis of defining the normative character of the Christian faith. It plays right into our culture's belief that "the new is true."

According to King we must "accept that the norm of early Christianity was theological diversity, not consensus." This is a very odd remark. How can theological diversity be a norm? A norm by definition is a litmus test or measuring rod, like a canon of Scripture, by which something is tried and found true or false. King seems to completely ignore the core beliefs about Jesus and his life, death and resurrection that united the earliest churches. These very things constitute the good news according to Paul (1 Corinthians 15:1-3). This was the tradition that Paul and other apostles passed down to the church. King also completely ignores masterful studies that examine the diversity of the early church and reveal that a King-espoused diversity was not the norm.

To the contrary, the early-church battle cry could have been *e pluribus unum*—"out of many, one." In 1 Corinthians 12:12-13 Paul says, "For just as the body is one and has many members, and all the members of the body, though many, are one body, so it is with Christ. For in the one Spirit we were all baptized into one body—Jews or Greeks, slaves or free—and we were all made to drink of one Spirit." And in Ephesians 4:4-6 he says, "There is one body and one Spirit, just as you were called to one hope of your calling, one Lord, one faith, one baptism, one God and Father of all." Notice the trinitarian flavor of this text, speaking of our relationship with Spirit, Lord and Father. The later councils didn't impose the divinity of

Christ or a trinitarian way of thinking about God on the church. The raw stuff, the beginning articulation of this way of thinking, is already seen in the New Testament. The earliest Christians are more characterized by what united them than by what divided them. It was this unity, this set of core beliefs, that made Christians stand out from other religious groups in the first century.

King is right that there were controversies and debates and differences among Christians in the first century. Indeed, the New Testament recounts this with candor and honesty. But to deny that the church was united by a core belief system is a total misreading of the history of earliest Christianity. This core is amplified and expounded on, not created, by the councils. The canon is simply the final outcome of the early collection and preservation of authoritative and apostolic documents.

But some will cry, Wait a minute. We don't have the original New Testament documents. All we have is copies of copies of these documents. What if the "orthodox" corrupted the Scripture before it was canonized? What if some monks surreptitiously changed the text while copying it so that now our New Testament is a far cry from what the original authors wrote?

THE ORTHODOX CORRUPTION OF SCRIPTURE

In 1997 Bart Ehrman published *The Orthodox Corruption of Scripture*. His area of academic specialty is New Testament text criticism—the study of ancient New Testament manuscripts to reconstruct what the original text said. We need textual criticism because we have none of the original copies of any of the New Testament books. Furthermore, even though we have close to five thousand ancient manuscripts of the Greek New Testament, no two copies are exactly alike. The question then becomes whether there was some sort of conspiracy to change the original readings of the New Testament to conform them to the orthodox theology of the fourth and fifth century church.

Ehrman meticulously explores what he calls the orthodox corruptions of

Scripture, and he is certainly able to document that scribes added to or subtracted from the text (usually the former) to *highlight* the true humanity or divinity of Christ. I emphasize the word *highlight* because Ehrman does not seem to be suggesting, as *The Da Vinci Code* does, that these ideas are simply imported into the text of the New Testament. For example, sometimes the word *Christ* is added to the name Jesus to highlight his exalted status from birth, but it is not as though a foreign idea is being imported into the text. The vast majority of these enhancements are not found in our modern Bible translations (for example, the NIV, NRSV and NLB) because the translators have accepted the conclusions of the text critics.

The most crucial type of "corruptions" are the ones that Ehrman thinks have made it into the canon. Some examples are (1) the adoptionist hints in Luke 3:22 (baptism), (2) Jesus' bloody sweat (Luke 22:43-44), (3) Luke's version of the Last Supper (22:19-20), (4) Peter's visit to the tomb in Luke 24:12, and (5) the title "Son of God" in Mark 1:1. Notice that the majority of these examples come from Luke. This is because there are two major manuscript traditions of Luke-Acts, the so-called Western text and the Alexandrian, or Eastern, text. The Western text is fuller and longer than the Alexandrian text.

Scholars have debated forever about how much weight to give the additional verses and readings found in the Western text. I am inclined to see most of them as not original to the Gospel of Luke or Acts. There is, for example, an antifeminist bias to some of these corrections or corruptions. (See, for example, Acts 18, where the Western text minimizes the role of Priscilla by either omitting her name or reversing the order of her name in conjunction with her husband's throughout the chapter, despite the fact that both are said to instruct Apollos). Ehrman may be right about some of the examples he cites, but even if we remove them from that Gospel, nothing major or substantive would really be lost to Luke's portrait of Christ as both human and more than human.

Perhaps the most important observation is that none of the "corruptions" are carried out in a systematic way. In other words, we have no evidence of a systematic conspiracy by the orthodox church to doctor the text of the New Testament, particularly the Gospels, in order to prop up a view of Christ that wasn't originally present in these texts. However, Ehrman does provide plenty of evidence that certain overzealous individuals were prepared to create forgeries to support their own view of orthodoxy. At the same time, there were numerous persons of integrity who, well before the canonization of the New Testament, believed that truth and the apostolic testimony did provide a criteria for evaluating the authority and usefulness of documents.

On the whole, Christian scribes were notably conservative in how they handled their data. Sometimes they were worried that one verse or another might be misunderstood, so they sometimes tried to clarify a meaning they thought wasn't apparent and might be overlooked. Sometimes they would find alternate readings in the margins of texts they were copying from and they included both readings. We get the sense that many of these scribes felt they were copying the holy book, the sacred Scriptures, and they didn't want to be careless and leave anything out that the originally inspired author had included.

In a helpful article G. N. Stanton has shown how even in the second century the Gospels were copied and treated as crucial, even as sacred, texts for public use in worship and evangelism. This can be seen by the extreme care and professional hand used in the copying. "The seven earliest papyri of Matthew suggest that this Gospel was used in both private and public settings; it was not considered by some of those who copied it and used it in the second half of the 2nd century to be of second class status." Stanton goes on to stress that this phenomenon when coupled with the widespread use of codices shows how revered and respected and authoritative these texts were already in the second century.

But if Ehrman had left his discussion at that point, there might not be any objection to his argument. However, he goes on to plow the very same furrow as Pagels and King. He too engages in revisionist history writing. When he deals with the environment of New Testament era Christianity, he argues for the very same sort of wide diversity of beliefs as Pagels and King do. In his view the struggle over an emerging orthodoxy wasn't solidified until the fourth century.

Ehrman then reviews the various church fathers' writings and polemical attacks against their opponents. He argues that the orthodox interpretation of their enemies as sensual, deviant deceivers and idolaters doesn't match the evidence. In this he is partly, though not entirely, wrong. Sometimes, when in attack mode, a church father would use rhetorical overkill, and their ad hominem arguments go too far. But Ehrman extends too much sympathy to those "opponents" and their views. What is more disturbing is the way that Ehrman implies that various church fathers were guilty of pure polemics in their evaluation of their opponents positions. Had Ehrman extended the same sympathetic reading to the church fathers as he does to their opponents, he might not have fallen so badly into the trap of misevaluating the earliest period of Christian history.

The polemics of the second and third centuries clearly demonstrate that various church leaders already had a very strong and clear sense of what was or wasn't in accord with the foundational documents of Christianity and the apostolic tradition. And they were prepared to argue for it. In other words, it is a myth to suggest that a faithful and true reading of the Christian tradition on a whole series of issues, especially regarding Christ, wasn't already established long before the Council of Nicaea. A good example of this is Bishop Serapion of Antioch (A.D. 190-211), who had originally let some of his flock read the *Gospel of Peter* in church. But when he read the book for himself and concluded it had a heretical view of Christ, he stopped its use. How much better Ehrman's book would have been if he had meaningfully interacted with many of Martin Hengel's works that deal with the history of both early Judaism and early Christianity.

HENGEL ON THE HISTORY OF EARLIEST CHRISTIANITY AND ITS SACRED TRADITIONS

Sounding an entirely different note from what we have heard from Pagels,

King and Ehrman, Martin Hengel's book *The Four Gospels and the One Gospel of Jesus Christ* is a detailed and rigorous analysis of *all* the relevant evidence about the development of Christian history and its traditions.

From the outset Hengel stresses that "Primitive Christianity has no knowledge of the abrupt distinction between 'dogmatics' and 'church history' which is so popular, or even between 'faith' and 'facts of history' in that form. . . . The truth lies between a 'historicism' which is hostile to theology and a 'dogmatism' which is hostile to history." Hengel is able to show that the titles of the biblical Gospels were in place by at least A.D. 125. This means that they likely circulated together because the titles were only necessary to distinguish one Gospel from another. Indeed, the collection of four Gospels may have been one of the first to circulate in one codex.

In *Books and Readers in the Early Church* Harry Gamble has shown that second-century Christians quickly took to the codex rather than individual papyri because it made circulating multiple documents easier. Gamble reveals that Paul's letters circulated in a collected form early in the second century. This isn't just because these documents were popular but because they were already seen as representative apostolic texts that faithfully presented the earliest and most authentic evidence and interpretation of Christianity. By A.D. 180 Irenaeus, in opposing things he deems heretical, speaks clearly and definitively about the fourfold Gospel (*Against Heresies* 3.11.7-9). In other words, in the second century Irenaeus already has a strong sense of what amounts to orthodoxy when it comes to the story of Jesus.

Even before Irenaeus, Justin Martyr calls the biblical Gospels the reminiscences of the apostles and says they were read and used in worship in the middle of the second century (*Dialogue with Trypho*, A.D. 160). Nothing comparable is said about any other "Gospels," not even the *Gospel of Thomas*. Irenaeus speaks quite specifically of how the four Gospels were composed by Matthew, Mark, Luke and John (*Against Heresies* 3.1.1). Equally important is the note in 2 *Clement* 2:4-5, a text from no later than A.D. 130, that calls a saying of Jesus ("I came not to call the righteous, but sinners" — Matthew 9:13, Mark 2:17, Luke 5:32) a word of Scripture.

One of the major mistakes made by the revisionist historians is that they focus too narrowly on the councils and fail to notice how portions of the New Testament are already being treated as Scripture long before the first council in A.D. 325. What Hengel is also able to show by close analysis of materials in Irenaeus and from Rome (for example, Clement of Rome) is that by the later part of the second century the four biblical Gospels: Acts; the epistles of Paul, Peter and John; and Revelation were being treated as sacred texts, and being quoted as if they were normative for the church. When we couple this with the Muratorian Canon, probably from the second century, we see that by the second century the church had not only begun the process of assembling sacred and authoritative texts but as also prepared to call them Scripture.

To be sure, there was continued debate about some of the General Epistles (Hebrews, James, 2 Peter, 2-3 John and Jude) well into the fourth century. But what is important is that debate implies criteria by which a document might be evaluated, criteria that included apostolicity, widespread use and orthodoxy. Lee McDonald says that in the second century the church may not have had a full-fledged canon of Scripture, but it used a canon of truth *(regula fidei)* to distinguish orthodoxy from heresy. The canon of Scripture came later as a legitimate and natural development of the canon of truth. We can say without hesitation that in the second century parts of the Eastern and Western church recognized the authority of some books that were to become part of the New Testament. By the early fourth century the authority of these books was without serious debate. Again, Constantine and the Council of Nicaea didn't impose their views about these documents on the church.

Determining which texts were sacred did not happen as a result of church councils. The church's hand was partly forced by the rise of heresies in the second through fourth centuries. Yet there was another impetus to establish the canon as well. Lee McDonald explains:

The final stages of the closing of the [New Testament] canon came in the early part of the fourth century during the empire-wide Diocletian persecutions in the years 303-313. This included the forcing of Christians to hand over their sacred writings to the Romans to be burned (see Eusebius *[Ecclesiastical History]* 8.2.1-5 for a description). When the persecution began, churches had to decide, if they had not done so already, which books were sacred to them and which could be handed over to the authorities. They tried to preserve the sacred Scriptures often by handing over to the authorities only the writings of lesser importance.

What is especially interesting about the canonizing process is not only how external factors pressured the church to make clear what they believed about these books, but equally noteworthy is the fact that when there were discussions about which texts should be included in the canon, the Gnostic Gospels and other Gnostic documents were never considered for inclusion. In fact, some of the books that did make it into the canon were heavily debated, and only a few other books (none of them from fringe groups such as the Gnostics) were considered—namely, the *Shepherd of Hermas*, *1 Clement*, the letters of Ignatius and, most surprisingly, the Jewish document Wisdom of Solomon! It is also noteworthy that not a single document written after about A.D. 120 was considered for inclusion, not least because such documents couldn't claim to be in direct contact with the apostolic tradition. This may explain in part why none of the Gnostic documents came up for debate. In all likelihood they are from a later date (the possible exception is the *Gospel of Thomas*).

The Gnostic documents weren't deleted from the canon, rather they were never serious contenders for inclusion in it. Only documents from orthodox writers were considered, and even many of those didn't make it into the canon. As the canon list of Athanasius (A.D. 367) demonstrates, even in the home region of the Nag Hammadi library, not one of those texts was included in a canon of sacred texts. They may have been copied, studied and read, but they never appear in any authoritative list, and it is also significant that when the Nag Hammadi texts were found, not one canonical book was among them.

Clearly, the evidence suggests that the canonizing process began at least in the second century. But is it possible that it began even earlier, in the first century itself? James D. G. Dunn has much to say on this matter:

The gospel about Jesus, the one sent from God, who died and was raised "for our salvation" was canonical more or less from the first. It defined and identified the new "sect of the Nazarenes." It gave canonical shape to the written expressions of the new faith, including not least the gospels. But it also determined, more or less from the start, what were *less than adequate* as expressions of that gospel. If there was a Q document containing only sayings, then it was valued as a collection of Jesus' teaching among the early Christian churches, though not as an alternative to the gospel. The argument that it was so conceived, that there was a Q "community," which knew only this form of Jesus' teaching and nothing of the gospel of Good Friday and Easter, or even was hostile to that gospel, is a scholarly hypothesis which confuses speculation with fact, and difference with antithesis. . . . There is nothing beyond scholarly imagination and contrivance to indicate that first-century diversity stretched much further than what is indicated by the New Testament writings themselves. . . . What if Q was dug up from the sands of Egypt? Would it not have to be included within the New Testament canon? No! Not at all! The decision was already made within the first century that Q should *not* be retained as it stood, but only as incorporated within the gospel form as we find in Matthew and Luke. . . . We should not forget the dynamic of the canon process. It is still sometimes assumed or implied that the New Testament writings did not function as canon until the church declared them canonical. This is simply an inadequate way to conceive of canon. . . . Rather we have to recognize that there were various writings which so impressed their first readers/hearers as church-creating and church-sustaining that they were retained by the recipients, reread, pondered, and circulated more widely. Something of this is already hinted at in the letters of Paul. In other words, they exercised a shaping, defining influence (a canonical authority) from the first. Not everything written by a Christian leader in the first century became canonical: some of Paul's letters, for example, were not retained; Q was not retained as Q. The fact that the New Testament writings were preserved is itself a testimony to the *de facto* canonical authority which they exercised more or less from the first. In short, the New Testament canon was not so much decreed as *acknowledged*. The New Testament writings were hailed as canonical in recognition of the authority they had been exercising from the first and in steadily widening circles since then. It is not the church that determines the gospel, but the gospel which determines the church.

Dunn goes on to say that when the church did get around to setting up a canon, it served the purpose not only of recognizing the limits but the range of acceptable diversity. However, this sort of approach to things was already implicit in the first century. In other words, limits were present from the outset, and this was formally acknowledged in the fourth century. Dunn says, "If the conviction that God meets us now through the one who was Jesus of Nazareth marks the beginning and heart of Christianity it also marks the limits and edge of Christianity." This Christ-centered and historical core is why, as Dunn himself says, the Gospel of John but not the *Gospel of Thomas*, the Acts of the Apostles but not the *Acts of Paul*, and the Apocalypse of John but not the *Apocalypse of Peter* were recognized.

WHERE DID THINGS GO WRONG?

In a particularly candid and confessional part of Elaine Pagels's beautifully written *Beyond Belief*, she speaks of how she had been "burned" by an evangelical church and alienated from the Christian faith while in high school. When a Jewish friend died, Pagels's fellow Christians told her the person was not born again and so was going to hell. This turned her off from the church, though not from the New Testament, which she studied in the

Greek in college. Then Pagels did doctoral work at Harvard. She recounts her reaction to hearing the Jesus saying from the *Gospel of Thomas*: "If you bring forth what is within you, what you bring forth will save you." She comments, "The strength of this saying is that it does not tell us what to believe but challenges us to discover what lies hidden within ourselves; and, with a shock of recognition, I realized that this perspective seemed to me self-evidently true."

This is an appeal to personal impressions or experience as the final authority. In such cases the person in question takes comfort from not being asked to believe specific things. The individual is the measure of truth, which is found within. Pagels's story is similar to the stories of many others. They tell tales of being turned-off by conservative churches. Sadly, some orthodox churches are the worst witnesses for orthodoxy.

But there is something else going on in Pagels's story, namely, the desire not to be told what to believe, not to be under the authority of others, not to submit to a truth that decidedly comes from outside herself. This isn't an uncommon reaction in a culture of individualism that resents institutions and prides itself on bucking authority figures. What we see in Pagels's often moving testimony of suffering and betrayal is a long, spiritual journey toward reconfiguring Christianity into a form of self-actualization. The Gnostic texts encouraged her to go in that direction. But this is just the opposite of the good news of Jesus, who says, "If any want to be my followers, let them deny themselves and take up their cross and follow me" (Mark 8:34). Or as Paul says, "I have been crucified with Christ; and it is no longer I who live, but it is Christ who lives in me" (Galatians 2:20). This is hardly a call to self-actualization or finding the light or truth within. Notice that in Mark Jesus doesn't say that we should deny ourselves something (for example, material goods, pleasure, etc.). It says we should deny *ourselves*. In the Pauline saying, the *self* is crucified.

Just how far afield Gnosticism leads becomes evident the further we get into Pagels's reflections on the *Gospel of Thomas*. She rightly observes how the Gospel of John differs from the *Gospel of Thomas*. In John the unity between a human ("I") and God ("Thou") involves an integral connection without the absorption of the one into the other. But in *Thomas* "I am Thou." The self is deified. For Pagels, theology has indeed become anthropology. I am the beginning and the end.

The problem with the advice "be yourself" or "be your own person" is that none of us are ourselves. We all have sinned and fallen short of God's glory, and we need the redemption Christ offers us, not another self-help program. We have fallen, and we can't get up on our own. Self-help programs don't turn us into new creatures even if they can help us curb our addictions or become kinder, gentler folks. Do we want to be ourselves as we are, or do we want to be something even better—to be like Christ and let Christ's life shine forth to others in such a way that they too will long to be like him? Elaine Pagels's story is an all-too-familiar and sad tale. And evangelical Christians need to take some responsibility for it because we fail to be winsome and Christlike.

READING BORG AGAIN FOR THE FIRST TIME

Marcus Borg is many things. He is a New Testament scholar who has made his contributions to the debates about the historical Jesus. He has been one of the more sane voices on the Jesus Seminar. He is an irenic person by nature and a good dialogue partner. He writes well and his seminars and church meetings are often packed out and lead to lots of profitable discussion. He and his wife, who is an ordained minister, are very involved in a church in the Pacific Northwest. He is also a person who presents himself as a Christian, though in a newfangled way. He is a goodhearted and sincere person who has been very candid about his own spiritual pilgrimage. Even though I think some of his ideas are wrong-headed and not in accord with the claims of the Bible, he has a winsome personality and is hard not to like.

Having discussed some of his work before in my book *The Jesus Quest*, I don't want to retravel that road. Instead, we'll look closely at his book *Reading the Bible Again for the First Time*, which is making its mark even as this book is being written. Borg's book brings to light precisely some of the things that are underlying the critique of early Christianity by Pagels, King, Ehrman, Brown and others. They no longer believe in the Bible as the revealed Word of God and so feel free to look in other directions for inspiration. Marcus Borg is merely saying out loud what others are assuming or presupposing. In his case, as in the case of others, the rejection of the Bible as a Word from God is what gives him permission to try to reinvent Christianity in an all-too-modern image.

The chief buzzword to look out for in the case of Marcus Borg is *experience*. Experience inevitably trumps the authority of the Bible when it comes to Borg's understanding of all kinds of things, including the plausibility of miracles (the resurrection of Jesus), the viability of ethics (issues such as homosexuality) and basic doctrine. The irony is that while Borg criticizes evangelicals and fundamentalists for being modernists and buying into the Enlightenment project in some ways, he keeps appealing to what modern people have experienced and are capable of believing. Modern beliefs about science and history and modern spiritual experiences seem to be Borg's canon, his measuring rod.

Borg doesn't seem to realize that when we make experience the ultimate guide, we have to be able to distinguish between good and bad, helpful and unhelpful, enlightening and deceiving experiences. Not all authentic experiences are genuinely good. But how can we tell the difference? Since none of us are omniscient, none of us can rule out the possibility that our own understanding may be too limited when it comes to judging subjective experiences.

MIRACLE WITH A CAPITAL M — THE RESURRECTION OF JESUS

In *The Resurrection of the Son of God*, N. T. Wright has taken on one of the major linchpins of Borg's critique of traditional Christianity, namely, that miracles never happen. Obviously, it only takes one genuine miracle in history to invalidate such a claim, and what better miracle to focus on than the bodily resurrection of Jesus? We will take a brief look at Wright's magisterial book on the resurrection of Jesus to see how he rules out the way Borg analyzes the resurrection—namely, as the visionary or purely subjective experiences of some early Christians.

It takes more than a little stamina to deal with a much-discussed topic as important and complex as the resurrection, particularly the resurrection of Jesus. Wright, however, is no fool rushing in where angels fear to tread. He stands on the shoulders of many others who have gone before him. The very scope of this work takes my breath away. Clearly, this work is the product of many years reflection and pondering and interacting with scholarly literature. It is the most exhaustive (and some would say exhausting) treatment of the subject currently available in English by any New Testament scholar. It deserves a thorough review and close scrutiny.

First, consider the scope and method of the work. Wright fully discusses every single significant and relevant passage from (1) the Old Testament and the New Testament, (2) early Jewish and early Christian literature from about 200 B.C. to A.D. 200, and (3) pagan literature. He marches through texts in an thorough manner, usually arranging them in a chronological order. Though we might think that Wright would start with the primary texts that deal with the resurrection of Jesus, namely the biblical Gospels, he doesn't. The first four hundred pages of the book examine what can be broadly called the Jewish and pagan background material and the Pauline material. The resurrection narratives themselves don't appear before page 587. So this book is about resurrection in general, *the* resurrection of Jesus in particular and the future resurrection of believers. Much ground is covered, but never in a hurried fashion.

Sometimes the flavor of a book can be determined by the scholars the author sides with and against, and this volume is an example of that tendency. Wright stands foursquare on the side of the orthodox view that Jesus rose bodily from the grave in a "trans-physical" body (one both like and unlike his previous body).

Wright has little sympathy for those who want to redefine the meaning of the term *resurrection* to assuage modern doubts and concerns. He contends that the primary meaning of *resurrection* is (1) not metaphorical but literal, (2) not referring to something that happens in the afterlife but to something that happens in space and time and history, and (3) not another way to talk about immortality of the soul but a statement about a body. Indeed, he stresses repeatedly that the resurrection flows naturally out of the doctrine of the goodness of creation, and that this is the way almost all orthodox Christians understood the term from the time of Jesus until well into the third century. Wright denies that there were any significant early forms or groups of Christianity that didn't believe in the bodily resurrection of Jesus, not the so-called Q community or anyone else. He doesn't accept the argument (largely from silence) that the Gnostic treatments of this matter should be seen as a legitimate or normal development of some aspect of the early Christian belief. This is so not only because the Gnostics denied the goodness of creation and its need for renewal but also because there is simply no good evidence that such persons and ideas were part of Christian communities before the second century A.D. And when they did appear in the second and third centuries, they were quickly opposed for offering an aberrant concept of resurrection. The theories of Elaine Pagels, Karen King and others have been tried and found wanting.

One of the strengths of Wright's argument is that he shows that the Pharisees' concept of resurrection is what was adopted by early Christians, though it was redefined around the person of Jesus and the surprising fact that he alone was raised on Easter. Wright says:

> "Resurrection," with the various words that were used for it and the various stories that were told about it, was never simply a way of talking about "life after death." It was one particular story that was told about the dead: a story in which the *present* state of those who had died would be replaced by a *future* state in which they would be alive once more. . . . "Resurrection" was a life *after* "life after death," the second of two stages in the post-mortem programme. Resurrection was, more specifically, not the *redefinition* or *redescription* of death, a way of giving a positive interpretation to the fact that the breath and blood of a human body had ceased to function, leading quickly to corruption and decay, but the *reversal* or *undoing* or *defeat* of death, restoring to some kind of bodily life those who had already passed through that first stage. It belonged with a strong doctrine of Israel's god as the good creator of the physical world.

Wright envisions then a two-stage process of afterlife. First, a person is absent from the body and present with Christ in heaven. Wright doesn't see this disembodied state as the final destination of Christians. The New Testament promises something better. Stage one is merely a way station before stage two—resurrection. Wright believes this temporary existence in the presence of God as compatible with the doctrine of resurrection, but he stresses that the Greek and Platonic concept of the immortality of the soul is definitely not what the New Testament means by resurrection. "This widespread belief in the future resurrection [of believers] naturally generated a belief in the intermediate state. . . . 'Resurrection' entails some kind of belief in continuing post-mortem existence; this need not mean a belief that all humans have an immortal soul in the Platonic sense, since the belief in YHWH as creator which is necessary for belief in resurrection is also a sufficient explanation for the dead being held in some kind of continuing existence."

Paul's letters, the earliest treatment of the resurrection in the New Testament, are critically important to Wright. He argues strongly that Paul never gave up his belief in the future resurrection of believers for a belief in postmortem life in heaven (not even in 2 Corinthians 4–5). The disembodied state is seen as a transitional condition on the way to the resurrection both early and late in Paul's letters (see, for example, Philippians 3:10-11). He also rightly argues that when Paul speaks of a "spiritual body" in 1 Corinthians 15 he does not mean a nonmaterial body. As the Greek form of the word *spiritual (pneumatikos)* itself suggests, it refers to a body totally energized and empowered by the Holy Spirit, not a body made of spirit (whatever that might mean). In other words there is no encouragement in the New Testament for talking about a nonmaterial resurrection. Indeed "nonmaterial resurrection body" would have been a contradiction in terms for early Jews and early Christians.

Wright demonstrates that it's not true that the Christian view of resurrection moved from a less to a more material view of what happened to Jesus. To the contrary, from Paul right through to the end of the early Christian period, resurrection always referred to a person coming back from death in a body. When it is used metaphorically about the Christian life (for example, in connection with baptism in Romans 6), it only makes sense as a subset of the physical resurrection and depends on it for its viability. Christians could now experience new life in Christ precisely because of the historical event of the bodily resurrection of Christ. Resurrection was not a way of describing life in heaven without a body.

In regard to the resurrection body's nature, Wright largely follows the lead of Paul in 1 Corinthians 15 in stressing there is both continuity and discontinuity between the old body and the new body. Wright correctly points out that resurrection texts like Daniel 12:2-3 do not come much into play in regard to the nature of the way the resurrection body is described in the New Testament. Neither Jesus nor Christians are described as becoming luminescent or becoming stars or angels. It seems clear that the New Testament description of the future resurrection body of believers is derived from the early descriptions of the properties of Jesus' resurrection body as recorded in texts like Luke 24 and John 20. At one juncture Wright tips his hand, revealing one major reason he is writing this weighty tome:

> The enormous pressure in some parts of the New Testament studies guild, particularly in North America, to come up with versions of early Christianity which know little and care less about the death and resurrection of Jesus, in order (dare one say) to legitimate similar movements today, or indeed to discredit movements which emphasize these things, should make us wary of hypotheses according to which an early version of "Q" provides evidence for that kind of movement.

Wright doesn't simply launch a theological argument in this work. He believes that on historical grounds it can be shown that Christians throughout the first century not only believed that Jesus rose bodily from the dead but that the actual Easter event itself, the resurrection of Jesus, is the one event that provides a necessary and sufficient explanation for the rise of Christianity.

Wright doesn't accept the argument of Borg and others that the New Testament merely claims that Christians had visionary experiences of Jesus after his death, that is, subjective impressions not grounded in objective historical events. He doesn't even see the resurrection of Jesus as being like the Transfiguration of Jesus, which seems to be more of a preview of the end rather than of the resurrection. He believes that the empty-tomb stories are part and parcel of the earliest Easter stories because *resurrection* meant something that happens to and in a body. He doesn't think that the empty-tomb stories alone could have generated the appearance stories or vice versa. The empty tomb alone could be explained in many other ways, including grave-robbing. The appearances, without an empty tomb, could have been written off as hallucinations. No, it is the combination of these factors that are involved.

Resurrection meant coming back to life from death in a body that could eat and drink and be touched (see John 20). But it was also, as Wright stresses, a transformed physical body no longer subject to disease, decay, death or the limitations of space that we currently endure. The "ruling hypothesis in much New Testament study, according to which the resurrection narratives were generated and developed as allegories of Christian experience, and then mistakenly read by subsequent generation as literal descriptions of concrete events, fails at the levels of literature, history and theology. The multiple meanings the stories have are multiplications of the basic point, and as with all multiplication you cannot start with zero." Wright also examines the early church documents that deal with the resurrection and shows quite clearly that the dominant tradition about resurrection lasted right into the Middle Ages.

The reference to the Son of God in the title of Wright's book, doesn't fully come into play until just near the end of the book. Wright argues that the resurrection demonstrates that God had vindicated Jesus' claims to be Israel's Messiah and the Son of God, the Lord over all the nations. He was indeed the embodiment of God's presence on earth. In other words resurrection not only undergirds but also underwrites the essential claims of the New Testament about Jesus as the Christ.

No one should make the mistake of dismissing Wright or his case by calling him a fundamentalist. This sort of ad hominem attack doesn't do justice to this fine scholar's work. Wright is both critical and respectful of differing opinions even when he attempts to dismantle them. Wright has thrown down the gauntlet and left us with a stirring challenge as he brings the volume to a close:

> What if the resurrection, instead of (as is often imagined) legitimating a cosy, comfortable, socially and culturally conservative form of Christianity, should turn out to be, in the twenty-first century as in the first, the most socially, culturally and politically explosive force imaginable, blasting its way through the sealed tombs and locked doors of modernist epistemology and the (now) deeply conservative social and political culture which is sustains? When I said that there was no neutral ground at this point, I was not only referring to patterns of thought and belief. Indeed, the holding apart of the mental and spiritual on the one hand from the social, cultural and political on the other, one of the most important planks in the Enlightenment platform, is itself challenged by the question of Jesus's resurrection.

The resurrection has, so to speak, been put back on the front burner once again. It will be interesting to see whose pots simmer and whose boil over as a result.

In light of Wright's incisive work it is both telling and a serious flaw that Borg basically skirts the issue of the resurrection in his new book. He limits himself to the comment that Jesus' followers in some sense *experienced* Jesus as a living reality after his death and gained the conviction that God has exalted him to be both Messiah and Lord. In a critical review of Borg's *Reading the Bible Again for the First Time*, Brian C. Jones says:

Presumably the emphasis falls on "experience" and "conviction" rather than on any extrasubjective act of God. His survey of the Gospels omits treating the resurrection accounts by focusing on the Gospels' inaugural presentations of Jesus and on a few select narratives from Jesus' ministry, a fact that must strike one as odd considering the centrality of the resurrection in Christian proclamation. Borg's readers might not have been comfortable being told plainly that the resurrection was a purely metaphorical narrative (it is hard to see how it could fit his category "metaphorized history"). The resurrection certainly qualifies as a unique and spectacular event with significant symbolic resonance and as such, by Borg's criteria, should be classified as a purely metaphorical narrative. . . .

In the New Testament it is clear that the early Christians did not think of the resurrection as an intersubjective event but claimed that objective witnesses had seen an empty tomb and seen (even touched and fed!) the resurrected Christ. These claims may be embarrassing and theologically problematic . . . but the embarrassment is not relieved by minimizing or ignoring them. The scandals of particularity and divine inconsistency cannot be removed from scripture without doing significant damage.

Unfortunately, the resurrection of Jesus is not the only essential tenet of orthodoxy with which Borg has problems.

THE BIBLE — GOD'S WORD?

In *Reading the Bible Again for the First Time*, Borg argues that Christians need to own up to the fact that the Bible is a completely human book put together by fallible human beings; thus the Bible is full of errors. Though the Bible is a testimony to the human search for God and truth, it's not a revelation from God to the world. To be more specific, he says the Bible isn't sacred in origin or inherently authoritative or truthful. It's "authoritative" only because the church has assigned this value to it and thus calls it

Holy Scripture. Rather, for Borg, the Bible is one vehicle through which we can experience or encounter God. This is a strange argument for someone who considers himself a Christian and believes that the Holy Spirit is leading him in his writings, and specifically leading him to be a prophetic witness to things he thinks are true about the New Testament.

In an age of biblical illiteracy, even within the church, it's not surprising that Borg has been invited to speak at many churches, and they have been listening intently to what he is saying. Clearly he has struck a chord with some Christians. And since he is a scholar with a winsome presentation, he has gained not merely a hearing but an audience. He seems to be the kinder, gentler version of the radical Bishop Spong, trying to help the church give birth to a new form of Christianity. But has the old, orthodox form of Christianity been tried and found wanting? Or is it just that the church is suffering from historical and theological amnesia? Did God inspire the biblical authors to speak the truth?

Our concern is not with Borg's particular analysis of New Testament texts but with his approach to interpreting them. From the very first chapter of his book it's clear that Borg wants to move the church beyond what he calls a fundamentalist (literal) reading of the Bible. Fundamentalists and evangelicals are basically lumped together under the heading of "conscious literalism," which includes a belief in the literal historicity and factual accuracy of the biblical story. Borg declares that he is challenging an understanding of Christianity that in his view is overly doctrinal, moralistic, patriarchal, exclusivistic and afterlife-oriented. This is not in accord with his understanding of "traditional Christianity" but rather is a product of the Reformation and the Enlightenment.

But in the end the true view of "traditional Christianity" is not the main question, rather the question is whether the fundamentalist and evangelical vision of Christianity works for "most of us in modern Western culture." He urges us to get beyond "fact fundamentalism to the realization that stories can be true without being literally and factually true." He calls the church to enter a period "beyond belief" so that we may focus more on our *experi-*

ence of God. It's not truth or truth claims that matter as long as we are having self-affirming religious experiences, hopefully with God.

It must be said that the first three chapters of Borg's book involve some very serious caricatures of fundamentalist and evangelical Christians. It is as if orthodox Christians have no literary sensitivity and couldn't tell the difference between poetry and prose, between parable and a historical narrative, between a riddle and a genealogy. No one who has actually read the works of many evangelical scholars or who has spent much time at evangelical colleges, seminaries and churches could possibly come to Borg's conclusion. His view isn't even an accurate portrayal of educated laypersons in conservative churches. He must assume that the liberal churches in the Pacific Northwest he's familiar with represent the intellectual majority of the church. But what evangelical churches has Borg been a part of, or has he been paying attention to what he hears when he's in conservative churches?

Of course it's true that stories can contain truths without being a recounting of facts. Such is the nature of parables. But it's a mistake to muddle history writing and parables or to come up with the hybrid category "history metaphorized." But Borg goes beyond this. He even argues that some narratives that appear to be historical accounts are actually purely metaphorical. The way we can detect metaphorized history is when (1) there is the presence of symbolic elements in the story that resonate with the culture and tradition of the context, and (2) there is the presence of spectacular events. Such stories, he says, "go beyond what we commonly think to be possible. . . . What I cannot do as a historian is to say that Jesus could do such things even though nobody else has ever been able to." He includes miracles such as walking on water, multiplying the loaves and fishes, turning water into wine, and the like. For Borg, these stories are purely metaphorical, without any basis in fact, though in his view they point to profound truths.

It's simply not true that only after the Enlightenment were Christians concerned about getting the facts straight about their faith. Early Christianity and early Judaism weren't founded on historicized parables and metaphors! These are historical religions founded on the belief that the mighty acts of God happened in space and in time. As Brian C. Jones says:

> Why are historical claims so important in the Judeo-Christian tradition? Simply because they are claims being made not only about the nature of God, which is a mystery. . . . *but also about the power of God*, which, to be credible by biblical standards, must be demonstrated within history. The rhetoric about the compassion and mercy of God displayed in the exodus and passion of Christ simply deflates if God has not in fact acted in some real, historical way. The texts make very clear historical claims that are valid only if the events actually happened. For the writers of the New Testament, the fact that Jesus' miracles are woven into the symbolism of the tradition does not diminish their historicity but rather substantiates it. . . . The claim that God has again acted powerfully in Jesus simply evaporates if metaphor entirely replaces history.

Facts were quite important to the writers of the New Testament; otherwise they could have been be accused of being purveyors of cleverly devised fables (though, of course, they weren't interested in facts alone). There is a vacuousness and indeed a danger of talking in generalities about the mighty acts of God unless the talk is linked to specific historical examples.

What is especially striking about some things Borg says is that what defines the limits of the possible or the miraculous is an unwillingness to go beyond what "we" commonly think is possible. In other words, Borg's modern assumptions about what can and can't happen set the limits to whether or not a miracle story from the ministry of Jesus is possible. But the experience of many persons throughout Christian history is that such miracles have happened and continue to happen. If Borg is going to make experience the bottom line, what about the many millions who have not experienced his "limits of the possible"?

What is so odd and paradoxical about Borg's argument is that while he criticizes evangelicals for having a worldview indebted to the Enlightenment, it is *he* who uses the Enlightenment critique of miracles to justify viewing much of the Gospels as nonhistorical. To this I say, "Physician heal thyself." More specifically, Borg needs to broaden his categories by spending more time with those who have experienced miracles in our own time.

Borg's dehistoricized, nonmiraculous perspective on the Bible impoverishes rather than enriches the way we read these texts. History plus more is surely more challenging, exciting and stimulating than metaphor minus history. Of course, as Borg says, we shouldn't attribute actions or miracles to Jesus that no one else has ever performed. But who is doing that? The book of Acts and Paul's letters as well as the chronicles of church history attest to miracles performed by many others. To take only one example, consider for a moment the testimony of Irenaeus that "we even raise the dead, many of whom are still alive among us, and completely healthy" (*Against Heresies* 2.32.4).

But what of Borg's suggestion that because our culture is moving rapidly toward a nonliteral view of the Bible, we should do the same? What culture is he referring to? Is it really true that "most" of us at the beginning of the twenty-first century find the older ways of reading the Bible unpersuasive? If he's talking about most churchgoing folks, he seems to be very wrong. George Gallup's recent religion surveys point in a very different direction. As even Borg himself admits, 62 percent of Americans (not just Christians but all Americans) have no doubt there will be a literal second coming of Christ, and even more believe it will probably happen! And why is it that as I am writing this book, millions are buying tickets to Mel Gibson's *The Passion of the Christ* if the miraculous heart of the Gospel is not believed by "most" Americans?

What Borg doesn't seem to appreciate about our postmodern situation is that people are not less prone, but in fact are more prone, to believe in miracles, magic and a host of other so-called nonrational things. It is true that postmodern people are more open to story, symbol and metaphor, but it isn't true that they are less open to supernatural events and experiences. It seems that only some of the jaundiced intelligentsia is close-minded about miracles and skeptical about historical claims. Borg is right that there is a new naiveté in our cultural situation, but that doesn't make people less open to miracles (and, unfortunately, all sorts of superstitions); it makes them more open to it.

The sad fact is that in our postmodern culture, where Jesus is a household name but most people are biblically illiterate, almost anything can pass as the truth about the historical Jesus. This is precisely why so many have been drawn to Borg's presentations. He offers them a user-friendly Jesus and a user-friendly Bible. But what people seem to be craving, to judge from the millions who went to see The Lord of the Rings movies and who have purchased tickets to see *The Passion*, is a reassurance that good will triumph over evil within human history. They long for an expansion, not an impoverishment, of their imagination and categories.

It's clear enough to me that Borg doesn't own up to his own indebtedness to the Enlightenment. For example, he insists that we must choose between seeing the Bible as a human product or as coming from God. Why the either-or? In a postmodern situation both-and is readily accepted. He argues that to accept the Bible as both divine and human leads to confusion. If the Bible is both human and divine, according to Borg, we are tempted to figure out which parts of the Bible are which, or we might take it all as divine revelation. In Borg's view the latter leads to morally and theologically unacceptable consequences—for instance, we might end up saying Jesus is the only way of salvation or that God condemns same-sex sexual behavior. Since that is unacceptable to Borg, he concludes that a more down-to-earth approach is required. The Bible doesn't tell us how it should be read, and so "it is we who must discern how to read and interpret, how to hear and value, its various voices." In other words we will bring our own theological and ethical agendas to the text, and they will guide us to value some texts and discard others. But this isn't even a matter of sifting out the more divine from the more human parts. In Borg's view it's always presumptuous to think God is speaking in and through these words of Scripture. Remember, the Bible isn't sacred in origin. The Bible becomes a critical dialogue partner with which we not only may but often must disagree "because we discern that they [that is, some of the teachings] were never the will of God." What criteria should we use to decide whether a biblical teaching is or isn't the will of God? In Borg's case it appears that things he has trouble coping with or has a hard time accepting can't be God's will. Strangely, Borg seems to affirm on the one hand that people have always had experiences of God, but he denies on the other hand that God could divinely inspire a human being to write sacred Scripture. Nevertheless, that God inspires Scripture-writing has been believed in almost every human culture from time immemorial. Yet Borg must deny these human experiences to draw the conclusions he does about the Bible.

THE BIBLE—INSPIRED BY GOD

From a strictly theological point of view, there is no problem with the notion that an omnipotent God could inspire even fallible human beings to accurately speak and write the truth for and about God. If indeed God can create the universe and raise Jesus from the dead, then inspiring people to speak the truth at least while under inspiration must be close to child's play.

Two things are particularly puzzling about Borg's denial that the Bible is God-breathed, as 2 Timothy 3:16 says. First, the truth of the Bible has been vindicated millions of times in the lives of the faithful and even in the lives of unbelievers, and second Borg knows perfectly well that there was a long tradition of prophetic inspiration going back well before the time of the New Testament and continuing long after it, a history I have chronicled in my book *Jesus the Seer*. The prophets rightly believed that when they said "Thus saith the Lord," they weren't merely speaking their own words, they were speaking God's Word through their own words.

Since Borg insists on appealing to experience as the litmus test, I will recount a personal experience.

In 1979 my wife Ann was pregnant with our first child. She is a biologist, which means that she knows far too much about all the processes in the female human body that go on during a pregnancy. We had gone to the

Lamaze classes in Durham, England, and we were determined to have this baby without the aid of drugs. We were going to have this child together, though in a hospital. Unfortunately, some weeks before our child was due, Ann's blood pressure elevated too high, and the doctor placed her on bed rest in Dryburn Hospital in Durham. On the night of August 13 I came to the hospital and Ann was distraught. The doctor had told her he was going to induce labor as her blood pressure was out of control. We had been reading through the book of Ezekiel for some time, and at that time we were in the midst of the doom-and-gloom chapters in that prophetic book. That night we were to read Ezekiel 36, and though there was still much doom and gloom in this chapter, there were also some promises—beginning at verse 8 we found promises that God would bring his people safely home, that he would multiply their kindred and they would prosper again, and that he would cleanse them of their impurities, such as the impurity of a woman's afterbirth. I looked at Ann and said, "Honey, don't worry, the baby is coming tonight." She said, "Really?" and I said, "God has just spoken to us and revealed it through his age-old Word." Of course I knew very well that that passage had been written for Israel in exile. I knew that Ezekiel had not spoken those words specifically for us and was not thinking of us when he wrote them down. But God brings to pass the revealed Word of God, including his oracles and prophecies, over and over again in the lives of his people in many different ways.

That night I went back to our home, the Methodist caretaker's cottage at our church, and paced the floor. I didn't go to bed because I knew that something was going to happen. I knew God had used that ancient prophecy to reassure us that all would turn out well, that just as the Israelites had returned home and prospered once more, so would my wife and I. Ann went into labor without any help at about 4 a.m. We had no car or phone, so she had someone call a friend to drive to our home, wake me up and take me up to Dryburn Hospital. Mr. Raymond was so surprised to see me fully clothed when I answered his knock on the door. "How did you know to be ready?" he asked. I told him that God had already told us the baby was coming and Ann would come home soon. A few hours later Christy Ann was born, alive and well with a head full of hair. But that's not the end of the story.

In the afternoon of that same day, August 14, 1979, I had gone back to the house to get a few things when a knock came on the door. It was two old friends, Tom and Marylee Albin, who had been living in Cambridge, England, and had gotten off the train on a whim to come look us up in Durham. The minute they looked at me they knew something was up. I eagerly told them about the birth of Christy. They said, "Wonderful, we will stay and cook and clean the church for you, so you can be with Ann and Christy." It's a hard thing to have a child overseas, far from family and friends. We weren't at home, and it didn't seem like home. But God's Word is true. He made that place a home on that day, not only by giving us a child who is now profoundly proud of having been born in England but also by bringing us Christian brothers and sisters to celebrate and be family with us.

KNOWING THE WORD'S WORTH

No one will ever convince me that the Bible isn't full of revelations from God. God's Word is trustworthy and true in so many ways. My long years of study, my intellect, my experience and my tradition have confirmed this. God's Word is powerful and pierces to the very heart of things. It is living and trustworthy, and not riddled with errors.

I am utterly convinced that the Spirit of God inspired the prophets and apostles and others who wrote these New Testament books. I am equally convinced that, as the Gospel of John says, the Holy Spirit inspires the readers or hearers to understand the Word; he convicts, convinces and converts their imagination, and leads them into all truth. More to the point, this is precisely what Paul and others believed was true about both the Hebrew Scriptures and their own inspired testimonies. Notice, for example, what James says in Acts 15: "It has seemed good to the Holy Spirit and to us" (verse 28) or what Paul says to the Corinthians: "what I am writing to you is the command of the Lord" (1 Corinthians 14:37). He says this because he is inspired by the Holy Spirit to speak the truth. The Holy Spirit is the Spirit of truth, not of error. The Spirit neither leads anyone to reject the Bible as the Word of God nor to contradict its essential theological and ethical teachings. The appeal to the experience of the Spirit is a good thing, but experience must be suspect if it leads a person to flatly contradict some essential teaching of the Bible.

The principles that Borg uses in interpreting the Bible are called a "hermeneutic of suspicion," that is, his approach to Scripture involves a failure of faith and nerve, as is shown by his failure to take seriously the historical and miraculous and demanding ethical content of the Bible. It's one thing to critique evangelicals for the faults they have. Indeed, Borg has aptly identified some of them. But it's quite another to throw the holy Book and the holy Baby out with the bath water. It's one thing to give the Gospel away to whoever will listen. But it's another to give away the Gospel only to replace it with a substitute that is less than good news for a sinful and suffering world. Instead, we need to operate with a hermeneutic of faith. As Johannes Bengel says, we should apply the whole of ourselves to the text and the whole of the text to ourselves. The moment we place ourselves, our reason or experience above God's Word as the final authority, we have started down a wrong road. Instead, we *must* place ourselves under the authority of the Word and ask God to lead us into all truth.

John Wesley encouraged his followers to use reason, tradition and experience as windows on and avenues through which to express the central truths of Scripture. He neither asked Christians to check reason at the door when interpreting the Bible nor to ignore the role that experience could play in validating biblical truth. He also treasured church traditions, creeds, confessions and the like. To call such distillations of truth "dry dogma," according to Wesley, is to miss their beauty and usefulness. And in part liturgy is both Scripture and dogma sung and said and prayed and confessed and pledged and promised. But in no case were reason or human experience or tradition equal in authority with the Bible on matters that it actually teaches and affirms.

In the end those who not only listen to Borg's view of the Bible but actually take it for Gospel truth are in danger of dishonoring the Word made flesh and the written Word. Like Esau, they have sold their birthright for a mess of pottage. Only in this case, the watered-down pottage has to be reconstituted and reheated for the ever-changing tastes of the culture. It's much better to taste and see that the Lord is good, and that his Word is like honey that nourishes the soul unto everlasting life (see Psalm 119).

WHAT IF GOD WAS ONE OF US?

About a decade ago there was a popular song sung by Joan Osborne, now used as the theme song for the TV show *Joan of Arcadia*, which asks:

What if God was one of us?
Just a slob like one of us
Just a stranger on the bus
Trying to make his way home

This is a good question, but notice the anthropomorphism that underlies the question. Anthropomorphism, in this case the attributing of human traits to God, has been going on as long as there have been human beings. The assumption is that God might be made in our image, that God might have our limitations and shortcomings, our propensity to search for home or a goal in life. There are both advantages and disadvantages to such an approach. Of course, it's good that God is personalized and is seen as approachable and someone to relate to. However, to attribute our shortcomings to God probably renders God incapable of helping us.

Perhaps it's no surprise that the most persistent form of anthropomorphism in our own sex-crazed culture is that of the "sacred feminine." The argument usually is made that in the patriarchal, male-dominated culture of the Bible God was assumed to be a male. This is a strange argument in some regards because in the Greco-Roman world of New Testament times, a world which was overwhelmingly male oriented, there were at least as many female deities as male deities. Indeed, some ancients complained that Olympus was overrun with such gods. The profoundly patriarchal nature of both Greek and Roman culture didn't prevent female deities.

Should we assume that because God is sometimes called "Father" in the biblical tradition, God is male? Should we assume, as is suggested in *The Da Vinci Code*, that the "sacred feminine" was suppressed in biblical culture?

GOD'S PERSONAL NAME

God's personal name is revealed to Moses in Exodus 3. This passage, particularly Exodus 3:13-15, has been a center of controversy in Old Testament scholarship. Of particular concern to us is how the divine name should be interpreted, and what this teaches us about God's character.

Prior to the revelation of God's personal name the Lord says he is the "God of your fathers, the God of Abraham, the God of Isaac, and the God of Jacob" (Exodus 3:6). The point is that Moses won't be asked to reveal to the Israelites some new God. Rather he is to speak to them in the name of the God of their own patriarchs. And beginning with verse 7 God explains that he hasn't ignored the cries of his people. Rather, God has both heard them and come down to do something about their suffering. God cares so much that he has come down to intervene on their behalf.

In verse 10 God says to Moses: "I will send you to Pharaoh to bring my people, the Israelites, out of Egypt." Moses' initial response is understandable—he is overwhelmed. "Who am I that I should go to Pharaoh?" God answers Moses with "*I will be* with you" (verse 12, emphasis added), perhaps a play on the name Yahweh as it is explained in verses 14-15.

Exodus 3:13-15 is the passage of greatest interest to us here. What sort of question is Moses asking when he asks for God's name (verse 13)? What does the name God reveals to Moses mean or signify (verse 14)? Moses' question is not merely hypothetical but is prompted by the natural and expected reaction of the oppressed Israelites. The authenticity of Moses' mission will be linked to a revelation of the divine name, confirming that God is *going to* act. Even though the first part of verse 14 has been traditionally translated as "I AM WHO I AM" *(ehyeh asher ehyeh)*, we know that *ehyeh* is an imperfect, which indicates a kind of action yet to be completed. In the case of verse 12, where *ehyeh* *a*lso appears, we know that the sense must be future ("I will be with you"). This suggests we should see it the same way in verse 14, meaning that it should be translated "I WILL BE WHO I WILL BE."

It seems probable that God's personal name, YHWH, is a shortening of the whole phrase *ehyeh asher ehyeh*. To be sure, this reveals something about God's name. The divine name then does not reveal the divine essence (who God is) but rather what Yahweh *will be* in relationship to his people. The Israelites need to know not merely that God exists but that God will act on their behalf. In his commentary on Exodus, S. R. Driver notes:

> The expression *I will be* is a historical formula; it refers, not to what God will be in Himself; it is no predication regarding His essential nature, but one regarding what He will approve Himself to others, regarding what He will shew Himself to be to those in covenant with Him, as by His providential guidance of His people, and the teaching of His prophets, His character and attributes were more and more fully unfolded to them.

The formula thus means "I will be understood by my future acts and revelation." Yahweh is the one who keeps intervening in human history.

This passage suggests that God will be known in what God will yet do—the divine nature being made plain by divine actions. God is a God of revelation, and therefore the future revelations and actions will further disclose the nature of God.

This narrative suggests an ongoing story in which God's people would look forward to and expect God to progressively reveal the divine character and plan and purposes. *One of the ways this happens is through the analogy between God's activities and that of a human father.* Thus God is even named Israel's "Father," the Creator and Sustainer of a people who relates to them in an intimate fashion.

THE GOD OF THE PATRIARCHS

The God of the Old Testament is revealed in various forms and under various names and images. Whether we think of the divine names Elohim or Adonai or the more personal Yahweh, it is striking that God is seldom directly named or prayed to as "Father" in the Hebrew Scriptures. Of course there are passages like Hosea 11, but even here the Hebrew word for "father" doesn't occur. Instead, an analogy is drawn between a good father's activities in his relationship to his son. The same sort of language appears in Psalm 103:13 ("as a father has compassion for his children, so the LORD has compassion for those who fear him"), and in Proverbs 3:12 we learn that God reproves those God loves just as a father reproves a beloved son. But we must distinguish between the use of paternal analogies and the naming of God as Father, especially because in the ancient Near East the name of a god connoted something real and vital about the nature of that God.

One possible case in the Old Testament where God actually may be named "Father" is Deuteronomy 32:6. In the "Song of Moses" we read:

Do you thus repay the LORD,
  O foolish and senseless people?
Is not he your father, who created you,
  who made you and established you?

The text refers to the relational nature of father language. One can't be a father without having one or more children. Thus as the Creator of human beings in general and the Hebrew people in particular, father language is quite natural. Yet as Walter Brueggemann stresses in *Theology of the Old Testament*, the father imagery does not necessitate a biological relationship here or elsewhere in the Hebrew Scriptures. Indeed, this language suggests something about how God *acts* in relationships, not about the essence of the divine nature.

THE GOD OF THE PROPHETS

This same sort of thing comes into play in Isaiah 45:9-11. A father is like a potter who has the right to shape his clay without giving an account to anyone else. So also the Lord, the Creator of a people, has the right to shape them as the Lord sees fit. The one reasonably clear exception to the Old Testament hesitancy to directly address God as "Father" is found in Isaiah 64:8: "Yet, O LORD, you are our Father; we are the clay, and you are the potter."

Malachi 2:10 also makes the connection between being a father and creating: "Have we not all one father? Has not one God created us?" In both cases the language connection between creating people and being their father is reasonably clear.

Several other prophetic texts also may be exceptions to the Old Testament demurral about naming God "Father." In Jeremiah 3:19 God's people are upbraided with the words: "I thought you would call me, My Father, and would not turn from following me." The implication is that God's people have *not* addressed God in this way, though it was something God had hoped for. Instead of having an intimate relationship with God, Israel was turning away from God and had ceased to follow God's ways. Jeremiah 31:9 also emphasizes that it is God's earnest desire to relate to his people as a father. He will protect those returning from exile, "for I have become a father to Israel."

Finally, there are a *few* texts where God is said to have a special father-son relationship with Israel's king. For instance, in the coronation ode of Psalm 2:7 we find: "You are my son, today I have begotten you." Though begetting language, which images God as father, is found here, it's used metaphorically for God's adoption of the king—in title and position he becomes God's son. Similarly, 2 Samuel 7:14 says of the king: "I will be a father to him, and he shall be a son to me." Psalm 89:26 says the king will address Yahweh as "my Father, my God, and the Rock of my salvation."

Having surveyed the few relevant references in the Old Testament, we can see why Walter Brueggemann concludes that images of Yahweh as "judge," "warrior" or "king" are far more prevalent in the Hebrew Scriptures. And when we do find father language, it connotes God's compassion and care, God's creating and sustaining roles in relationship to Israel or God's adoption of Israel's king as son. The father image for Yahweh "provides a way in which Israel can speak about Yahweh's profound commitment to Israel, a commitment on which Israel can count for special, positive attention." However, Brueggemann explains, it

> is evident that the father, while tender and generous, is not romantic about the relationship but is capable of regret and fierceness. In Jer 3:19 and 31:15 and Hos 11:1-9, the metaphor of father is employed in order to exhibit the tension between fierceness and compassion in the inclination of Yahweh. In these texts, as in Psalm 103, Yahweh's compassion prevails.

Yahweh then is father in the sense that the Lord alone, as Creator, makes Israel's life possible, and has a close relationship with and concern for Israel as a people, and especially with their king.

Compared to other ancient Near Eastern cultures of the time and the New Testament, the ancient Hebrews rarely addressed God as father. But why? This contrast has suggested to Willem A. VanGemeren that

> Israel was surrounded by nations who held to a mythological understanding of a relationship between the worlds of the gods and men. In this context the writers of the [Old Testament] cautiously referred to Yahweh as "Father." Yahweh is not El, the father of "the gods." He is not Baal, the god of fertility. Yahweh is the Creator of everything and is sovereign (Lord, King, Ruler) over the nations.

This explanation is likely partially correct, but then why wouldn't the early Christians have avoided such language as well? They were all initially Jews, and in their day father language was still being applied to numerous gods who begat other gods, and to the emperor himself. Perhaps we could hypothesize that since Christianity was a missionary religion, it actually looked for points of contact with the God language of the larger culture, whereas Hebrew God talk was primarily concerned with stressing what distinguished Yahweh from other deities. But the language use of surrounding cultures can't entirely explain the absence of father language in the Old Testament.

In his book *Word Without End,* Christopher Seitz says we need to take into account the perspectival difference in the use of *father* in the Old and New Testaments. In the Old Testament things are seen from the Father's point of view, whereas the Father is largely viewed from the Son's point of view in the New Testament. In other words the "change . . . has less to do with matter of culture, *or even something more personal or psychological,* and more to do with the appearance of the man Jesus and a change in perspective: from The Son to YHWH, who is referred to from that filial point of standing as 'Heavenly Father.'" I think he is essentially correct. Jesus himself places the emphasis on God as Father, and this explains why *Father* is so much more prevalent in the New Testament. The relationship of Jesus to the Father changes the way his followers look at God.

Another answer sometimes offered is that the Israelites, with very few exceptions, did not have an intimate relationship with God in the same sort of familiar or familial terms as early Christians did. Therefore the fatherlike character of God wasn't fully revealed to Israel. Yahweh was prepared to relate to Israel in this way, but they were not prepared to respond in such terms. In fact notice in the prophets father language is used to chastise Israel for moving away from the possibility of such an intimate relationship. Yet in this later prophetic literature God's fatherlike character begins to be more fully revealed, and this progression continues on into the intertestamental literature. It is as if God was increasingly revealing the divine nature in intimate terms, not just to individuals but to the chosen people as a whole. Nevertheless, father language in Israel remained muted. So God as Father in the Old Testament is not as prevalent or as important as some critics may suggest.

GOD IN THE INTERTESTAMENTAL WISDOM LITERATURE

Further development of the Jewish use of father language for God is revealed in the intertestamental Wisdom literature, for example Wisdom of Solomon 14:3; Sirach 23:1, 4; 51:10; and 3 Maccabees 6:3, 8. Especially striking among these texts is Wisdom of Solomon 14:3, where God is actually addressed as "Father." This may suggest a growing tendency, first noted in the later prophetic books of the Old Testament, toward using such language of God. This trend continues in the New Testament. Also in some of the Qumran fragments (4Q371-372) God is sometimes addressed with the formal "my father." Thus it appears that there was a growing trend in Jewish culture to address God as "Father." In addition, material in the later Jewish writings and commentaries points to a growing use of father language for God. Nevertheless, Jesus' use of the Aramaic *abba* remains without parallel.

What may we conclude from this cursory exploration of father language for God in Jewish literature? First, it seems quite apparent that there is evidence of intimacy between God and the chosen people in this literature. God repeatedly attempts to treat the chosen people as a good father would his children. The father language is especially used in relation to the creation of the chosen people.

Meye Thompson claims that the Jewish naming of God as "Father" is not derived from attributes that are inherent to the male gender "but, rather, from a specific set of functions which were appropriate to fathers in that Israelite culture." But this is not totally correct. To the extent the term is used to describe God as a *begetter* rather than a *conceiver* of creation, there is a gender-specific component to the term. Only males beget, only females conceive. This doesn't mean Yahweh should be thought of as a male when he is called "Father" but that *Father* sometimes refers to some gender-specific activities. In other words, in such cases *Mother* would not be equally suitable. We will see that this is also true in the New Testament when God is described as the Father of the Son, particularly where the context makes clear that Jesus didn't have a human father who begat him (see Matthew 1 and Luke 2).

Remember that using father language of God is rare in the Old Testament. Father language was mainly used by special individuals who had a personal relationship with God. Yet there seems to have been an increasing degree of comfort with father language as we get to the late prophetic and the intertestamental period. God as Creator and parental guardian and guide of a people are the images that come to light from the use of father language in this period. However, there is no clear evidence in the early Jewish literature for praying to God as *abba* prior to the time of Jesus. As we turn to the New Testament, we discover a remarkable proliferation of father language, which reveals new information about God. God's story takes a dramatic new turn when Jesus the Son appears.

In summary, in the Old Testament and intertestamental literature we didn't find the following things:

• the use of *abba* as an address for God in prayer

• the regular use of "Father" or *abba* by a particular historical individual to indicate a personal relationship to God

• any adequate historical explanation (based in pre-Christian usage of father language) for the astonishing proliferation of father language for God in the New Testament, which were almost all written by first-century Jewish Christians,

• any adequate explanation for why the use of father language in early Christianity seems to have increased from the time of the writing of the earliest Gospel (Mark—which has only four references to God as Father) to the time of the writing of the later Gospels (particularly Matthew, which has more than 30 references to God as Father, and John which has some 120 references)

All of these factors reveal that the early Jewish context by itself can't explain the New Testament's use of *Father* or *abba* for God. So what happened?

JESUS, ABBA AND THE SON'S RELATIONSHIP TO THE FATHER

Earlier, I noted that a probable explanation for the difference in use of father language in early Judaism and early Christianity, and it has to do with Jesus. As Christopher Seitz argued, the Old Testament views things from the Father's perspective, but theFather is largely viewed from the Son's point of view in the New Testament. This is essentially the correct answer.

Jesus himself places the emphasis on God as Father, and this explains why the New Testament uses father language so much more than the Old Testament. More important, the new perspective of seeing the Father through the eyes of the Son and through the Son's relationship to the Father explains what we find in the New Testament. This special relationship is presaged by the language to describe the king's relationship with God, for example in Psalm 2. In other words, the special relationship Israel's anointed one, the king, was to have with God provides some precedent for Jesus' use of father language, not the occasional and more general use of father imagery to describe the relationship of God to Israel in general. Christians came to believe that individuals come to the Father through Jesus the Son in part because Jesus had a special sonship relationship with God the Father. Jesus acted out the drama of being God's anointed one and mediated this new relationship with the Father. Jesus didn't see himself as Israel but rather as Israel's Redeemer, and indeed as the agent and emissary of the Father.

In his *New Testament Theology* Joachim Jeremias argued that "the complete novelty and uniqueness of *'Abbā* as an address to God in the prayers of Jesus shows that it expresses the heart of Jesus' relationship to God." Jeremias didn't maintain that Jesus' view of God was entirely novel but that his mode of address to God was novel because his relationship with God was distinctive. In other words, neither the texts that manifest a corporate relationship to God (for example, later rabbinic prayers addressing God as "our Father") nor the general use of father imagery to describe some activity of God are true parallels to Jesus' use of Father.

The term *abba*, clearly enough, is an intimate way of addressing God using family language, whether by a child or an adult, and as such is less formal than addressing God simply as "God" or "Lord." Jeremias's main point is that Jesus' choice of this term reveals Jesus' awareness of his special relationship with God.

After Easter, God is addressed in intimate terms by Jesus' disciples because God has drawn near through Jesus in a definitive way, creating a familial relationship with the disciples that didn't fully exist prior to Jesus. In other words, while the Old Testament reveals God's longing to have a familial relationship with his people, it wasn't until the ministry of Jesus that this relationship was fully revealed and enacted. Paul discusses *abba* in the context of the final saving work of Christ and the Spirit, which reflects the impact of Jesus' use of *abba*. We may conclude then that there is more than sufficient evidence that Jesus himself prayed to God and addressed God as *abba* or "Father." Thus it's apparent Jesus had an intimate *relationship* with God. At Gethsemane he pleaded with God as a Son to his Father, addressing him as dearest Father *(abba)*.

We could also examine the Q material in Matthew 11:25-27 (see also Luke 10:21-22) and Matthew 7:9-11 (see Luke 11:11-13), the parable of the vineyard in Mark 12:1-12, and the parable of the prodigal son (Luke 15:11-32). Through these an intimate relationship between the Father and Jesus is clearly depicted.

If we put all these insights about Jesus' use of *abba* together, a compelling picture emerges of the Father whom Jesus knew intimately. For Jesus, God is *abba*, whose will and word is final. But this Father is no harsh, unforgiving figure. To the contrary, the Father's active care, compassion and forgiveness is a repeated theme. We come to know and respond to the Father through the Son, the final emissary to God's people. The prevalent use of father language for God in the early church had two sources: (1) Jesus' own use of such language and (2) Jesus' intimate and special relationship with the Father. Both Jesus' father language and his relationship with the Father had an enormous affect on the early church.

PAUL AND THE FATHER OF THE LORD JESUS CHRIST

The earliest written documents in the New Testament are, according to the vast majority of scholars, Paul's letters. These letters give us the earliest windows on the faith of the early Christians and particularly on their relationship with God.

As James D. G. Dunn made clear in his *Jesus and the Spirit*, for Paul the gift of the Spirit of God to believers in Christ is the first part of the redemption of the whole person. The Spirit enables us to make a true confession that Jesus is the risen Lord (see 1 Corinthians 12:3), and the Spirit enables us to pray to God as *abba*. By the Spirit the presence of God replicates the life of Jesus in his followers' lives, conforming them to Jesus' image. This includes enabling the believer to have the same sort of prayer life and intimate relationship with God as Jesus did. Indeed the presence of this Spirit conforms us to the image of Jesus such that we become sons and daughters of God, somewhat analogous with Jesus' being Son of God. Paul goes even further, suggesting that the presence of this Spirit not only prompts prayers like Jesus' prayers but enables us to become fellow heirs with Jesus (Romans 8:17).

There are at least forty references to God as Father in Paul's letters. Every one of the Pauline letters begins with some form of greeting or opening blessing that refers to God as "our Father," "the Father" or more expansively "the Father of our Lord Jesus Christ." Meye Thompson has rightly pointed out that the references to God as Father in Paul's letters tend to be found in the opening remarks, in benedictions or in quotations. What these observations suggest is that Paul tends not to use father language outside of his source material or liturgical contexts (prayers, blessings, benedictions). Such language was already prevalent in the sources and worship contexts Paul was familiar with, and he simply echoed what he found there. This fact also strongly supports the idea that we can't attribute the proliferation of father language in early Christianity to Paul.

Paul's use of father language reflects the new situation that began with the arrival, death and the resurrection of Jesus. God isn't referred to as "Father" when Paul speaks about the heritage and future of Israel in Romans 9–11. Nor is God's fatherhood related to Abraham in Romans 4. The story of Jesus, not the story of Israel, undergirds the references to the fatherhood of God in Paul's letters.

Paul's use of father language provides further justification for thinking that the earliest Christians referred to God as they did because of the way Jesus referred to God and because of what was true about Jesus' relationship to the Father. They believed that they had become adopted children of God because of the Son of God, and they had access to the Father through the Son. Indeed, they believed that in an analogous fashion the Spirit replicated the prayer life of the Son in them. They also believed that while they didn't have independent access to the Father, they had that access through the Son and by means of the Spirit. Thus through the Son and the Spirit they had come to have an intimate relationship with God.

THE FATHER IN MARK, LUKE AND MATTHEW

The Gospel of Mark. There are only four references to God as Father in the earliest Gospel, one of which, Mark 14:36, is in the garden of Gethsemane. In the second text, Mark 8:38, there is the reference to the Son of Man coming in the Father's glory. A third text is found in Mark 11:25, where the Father in heaven is said to forgive our trespasses, provided those who pray for forgiveness also forgive their fellow humans. If Mark 8:38 stresses the glory of the Father, this text stresses the compassion and forgiving nature of the Father. There is no precedent for this in the Old Testament or in the literature of early Judaism, and thus it appears to strike a new note in understanding how the Father operates. A fourth text is Mark 13:32, which indicates that there is a distinction between the Father's and the Son's knowledge (at least during the Son's earthly ministry).

Overall, the portrait of the Father in Mark is of an omniscient, omnipotent and omnibenevolent deity who has a special relationship with the Son. This relationship involves shared glory, shared knowledge (to some extent), shared power and a common commitment to the will of God. Jesus, conforming his will to the Father's, could turn to the Father in his darkest hour and be heard because he is the beloved Son (Mark 1:11; 9:7).

The Gospel of Luke. Like Mark, Luke doesn't frequently use father language. It's found only seventeen times in the Gospel and only three more times in Acts (Acts 1:4, 7; 2:33). As Meye Thompson stresses in *The Promise of the Father*, all references to God as "Father" in Luke-Acts are in Jesus' own speech, with one exception. The proper conclusion to be drawn from this is that Luke not only sees father language as characteristic of Jesus but as a distinctive of his discourse. Only the leader of the Twelve, Peter, is portrayed as using the father language as Jesus did, and only after Pentecost (Acts 2:33). No text portrays any disciple using such language before Easter even though Jesus instructs his disciples to pray this way at Luke 11:2. This comports well with the stress in Luke 10:22 that no one knows the Father except the Son.

The overall portrait of the Father in Luke-Acts is of an extremely compassionate, forgiving God who gives both material and spiritual blessings. But the fact that only Jesus speaks of God as "Father" during his ministry and only Jesus truly knows the Father and can reveal him shows that Luke believes Jesus had a distinctive, indeed unique and unprecedented, relationship with the Father. Once the promise of the Father, namely the Spirit, is bestowed, the disciples can in a derivative sense speak of God as Father. This Father-Son relationship is neither a relationship shared between Israel and God nor simply transferred in toto to Jesus' disciples. Only the presence of the Spirit in the believer's life enables an approximation of such an intimate relationship.

The Gospel of Matthew. When we turn to Matthew's portrait of the Father, we are immediately struck by the abundance of references to the Father in contrast to what we find in Mark or Luke-Acts. Matthew uses father language for God more than Mark and Luke together. More often than not "Father" is prefaced by some sort of possessive ("my" or "your") in Matthew's Gospel (compare, for example, Matthew 26:39 to Luke 22:42). Whereas Luke has "my Father" four times, Matthew has it fourteen times, and while Luke has "your Father" three times, Matthew has it fifteen times. (Significantly Luke's Gospel, in terms of numbers of Greek words and lines, is a bit longer than Matthew's.)

Meye Thompson compares parallel passages of Matthew's and Luke's use of Q and Mark: (1) where Matthew 6:26 has "your heavenly Father," Luke 12:24 has "God"; (2) where Matthew 10:20 has "Spirit of your Father," Luke 12:12 has "Holy Spirit"; (3) where Mark 3:35 and Luke 8:21 simply refer to "God," Matthew 12:50 has "my Father in heaven"; (4) while Mark 14:25 and Luke 22:18 refer to the "kingdom of God," Matthew 26:29 refers to "my Father's kingdom." Stephen C. Barton is surely right that "for Matthew, God's presence is experienced as fatherly."

Meye Thompson observes, "Matthew still retains the singularity of Jesus' address to God as 'my Father' and his admonitions to his disciples regarding obedience to 'your Father.' Clearly there is a distinction between the way in which Jesus relates to God as Father and the way in which the disciples do. Matthew's manifest predilection for the formulation 'my Father' reflects his understanding of the distinctive character of Jesus' Sonship and the relationship of the Father and the Son." This is a correct observation, but it is also observed in Paul, in Mark and even in the material that goes back to the historical Jesus. It is just that Matthew highlights this more, as does the Fourth Evangelist.

In Matthew we see a pattern emerging—the more Jesus' divine nature is highlighted in a New Testament document, the more likely there is to be a strong emphasis on the Father's relationships with Jesus and others (not merely a greater frequency of father language). The more focus on the Son, the more focus on the Father as well, to make clear the distinctive relationship the Son has with the Father. The Father is "the Father of our Lord Jesus Christ," and this is one of the main things that distinguishes this Father from other deities (or emperors) that might be called "father." In addition, the more emphasis on Jesus as the means of salvation, the more the emphasis on human beings relationships with the Father going through the Son. One comes to the Father of Jesus through Jesus. This comports with the suggestion that in the New Testament the Father is seen through the eyes of the Son and is related to by means of one's relationship with Jesus.

All such discussions are grounded in the intimate relationship between the Son and the Father.

THE FATHER OF THE WORD IN THE GOSPEL OF JOHN

When we reach the Gospel of John, we reach the apex of the use of father language for God in the Gospels. In fact here for the first time *Father* is used more frequently than even the term *theos* ("God"). John refers to God as Father about 120 times, and he uses *God (theos)* 108 times. It is crucial to bear in mind that the Gospel of John is oriented around Christ's divinity, and this orientation is set in the prologue. This Gospel is about the preexistent Word who took on flesh and dwelled for a time with human beings. In John 1:14-18, where the subject of the incarnation is broached, we hear for the first time about the Father. The people witnessed the glory of the Father's only-begotten *(monogenēs)* Son. The point is that this Son comes directly from the Father, who is the begetter. That is, Jesus is not an adopted Son of God. Just like produces like, so the Father produces the Son. He is not inherently distinct from the Father. Thus there is a clear distinction made between the only begotten, or "natural," Son and those who become children of God by belief and response to the Word.

As was the case with the first three Gospels, references to God as Father in the Fourth Gospel come almost solely from Jesus. Indeed only Jesus addresses God as "Father" in this Gospel. He speaks of "my Father" (about two dozen times), "the Father" (more than eighty-five times), "holy Father" (once) and simply "Father" (eight times). But unique to John is "the Father who sent me."

Jesus neither uses the phrase "our Father" nor does he teach the disciples to pray this way in this Gospel. Meye Thompson observes:

> What is particularly telling in the depiction of God as Father is the way in which God's actions as Father are focused on Jesus himself. It is Jesus who speaks of, and addresses, God as Father. Jesus speaks but rarely even to his own disciples of God as their father, and then only

after the resurrection. In short, according to [John's] Gospel it is the prerogative of Jesus to address God as Father and speak of God in these terms.

In this Gospel the theological implications of Jesus' use of father language are made clear at various junctures. For instance, in John 5:17-18, where Jesus says, "My Father is still working, and I also am working," we are told that some Jews sought to kill him because he was "calling God his own Father, thereby making himself equal to God." Jesus, according to the Fourth Evangelist, was definitely claiming some sort of distinctive status and relationship with the Father.

It can't be overemphasized how much John stresses the unity and love and intimacy between the Father and the Son. The mutual affection between the Father and the Son comes up multiple times (John 3:35; 5:20; 10:17), but only once is it said that God loves the world (John 3:16) or that the Father loves the disciples (John 16:27). Notice, though, that *God* is used when talking about the love of the world, whereas *Father* is used when the text refers to the love of the disciples. The family relationship doesn't exist between God and the world even though he loves the world. People must first become children of God through faith before God is truly their Father, according to this Gospel, and that entails first having a relationship with Jesus.

The Son is the way, the truth and the life in matters of salvation. Those who know the Son also know the Father, for the Son is the very image of the Father (John 8:19). "The 'kinship' of God and Jesus as Father and Son becomes the basis for a number of claims made for Jesus. These claims include his authority to judge, to give life, to mediate knowledge of the Father and to reveal him, to do the works and will of the Father, and therefore to receive honor, as even the Father does." All that Jesus does pleases the Father (John 8:29). And the Father testifies on behalf of Jesus, glorifies Jesus and gives all things into Jesus' hands (John 8:18, 54; 3:35).

More could be said along these lines, but this is sufficient to make clear

that the higher the reflection on Christ, the more likely the proliferation of
father language for God. It's not necessary to trace this discussion any further in the New Testament. Having dealt with the most pertinent evidence,
suffice it to say that the rest of the New Testament brings little new to light
and only confirms what we have already noted.

EXPLORATIONS AND IMPLICATIONS

Contrary to what some scholars say, there is very little evidence to support
the proposition that the proliferation of father language in the New Testament comes (1) from the influence of the Old Testament or early Jewish
uses, or (2) as a residue of the general patriarchal culture or pagan practices
(for instance, the emperor cult). To the contrary, the evidence we have
strongly suggests that the Christian use of father language derives from
Jesus' own use and reflects the growing emphasis on the divine nature of
Jesus Christ. The Father is seen through the eyes of the Son. God the Fa
ther is most often referred to as Jesus' Father or the Son's Father and, in a
derivative sense, as the believer's Father. On rare occasions *Father* refers to
God as Creator of all.

One of the important motifs behind father language is the notion of the
Father as a begetter of the Son and, in an extended sense, of believers who
are "born of God." Begetting is a gender-specific function, and thus it is
simply untrue to say that when applied to God, father language doesn't
predicate of God any gender-specific functions. While probably the majority of references in the New Testament to God as Father have to do with his
love, mercy, compassion and the like (that is, being a good parent to his
people), the New Testament consistently equates Father and Creator. Specifically this means the Father is the begetter; particularly the Father begets
the Son, which is made most clear in the Fourth Gospel.

Thus Jesus set a precedent of calling God *abba*, or Father, that provides
an important warrant for Jesus' disciples to use such language. However,
even more, there is a theological rationale for Jesus' use of such language;
namely, he believed God truly was the one who, along with Mary, gener-

ated his human nature through a miraculous virginal conception. Clearly enough two of the Gospel writers also believed this to be true.

This belief could explain why Jesus speaks repeatedly, as no one else did, of "my Father" in heaven. Furthermore, it becomes apparent Jesus couldn't call God "Mother" precisely because he had a human (biological) mother. In other words this choice of language ultimately comes out of the unique relationship Jesus had with the Father, a paternal relationship. And by another miracle, the miracle of being born of God, believers have an analogous relationship to the Father.

None of this is meant to deny that in the biblical tradition female language is sometimes used to describe God's (and Jesus') actions. Such language may also reflect the fact that God is spirit, neither male nor female. Then why is God named and characterized as Father but not Mother in the New Testament? The answer is related to Christ's nature and his being the font of Christian practice in regard to calling God "Father." It doesn't appear to be related to either patriarchy or the competing religious practices of non-Jews. The answer also has to do with the role God plays in the new birth of believers.

Some people complain that the use of father language is insensitive to those who have come from abusive and dysfunctional relationships with their human father. Donald Juel explains:

> Many within the Christian family . . . cannot speak the opening words, "Our Father," without some intense experience of alienation. It is not only women who may have difficulty speaking the words; there are men who have no sense that there is a "Father" behind the dim unknown keeping watch above his own, and there are many who have no sense of the "we" presupposed by the Prayer. Language that earlier generations might have taken for granted may now require attention if the Prayer is to serve as a vehicle for conversation with God.

There are however serious theological problems with determining what God language we use on the basis of relational problems or dysfunction. Of course we always need to be sensitive to people who have been abused, but our naming of God should not be dictated by such human dilemmas. The appropriate response is that there are good human fathers as well as bad ones, and analogies should be drawn with human relationships at their best, not their worst.

Neither Jesus nor the New Testament writers say what they do about God the Father because of what they know to be best about human fathers. Their discussion is grounded in a particular set of historical relationships: (1) the relationship of Jesus with God, and (2) the relationships of early Christians with God made possible by Jesus and enabled by the Holy Spirit. The Father is seen through the eyes of the Son and on the basis of his words and actions. After receiving the Spirit at Pentecost, the disciples began to call God "Father" as Jesus instructed them to.

So what's wrong with *The Da Vinci Code* and its discussion of the "sacred feminine"? Several things. There is no evidence of the suppression of the divine feminine in Israel. God was never spoken of or conceptualized in that way in Israel because God is spirit, neither male nor female. The physical manifestation of God's presence in Israel was never viewed as a female deity. Yes, there were some Israelites who lapsed into pagan practices, but this was always viewed as an act of infidelity. The problem with re-creating God in our own image is that we inevitably get it wrong. God is not a "blob" on a bus trying to find a way home. God is the Creator and Redeemer of the universe.

God is called "Father" because he is the begetter of the only begotten Son. And by the divine action of the Creator God, the Father of Jesus, those who love Jesus receive status as sons and daughters of God. In other words, father language is a testimony to the remarkable grace of God in transforming Jesus' followers into something more nearly like the divine image. We can't do this for ourselves through special knowledge, secret rituals or sacred sex. We have no capacity to divinize ourselves or even make ourselves into all that we ought to be. We need to be saved and renewed by the Holy Spirit before we can genuinely cry out "*Abba*, Father." When we give up the quest to divinize ourselves, the quest for our own personal holy grail, we are paradoxically transformed by God—making us into the image of God's Son. The Son is the means by which God saves the world.

The holy One is neither "sacred feminine" nor "sacred masculine." His name (Father) isn't derived from patriarchal presumptions or practice; it comes because Jesus called God "Father" and because God alone can remake human beings, transforming and renewing the marred image of God within us. God does this through Jesus Christ. This indeed is good news! May we never lose hold of these truths in these spiritually dangerous times.

TRUTH DECAY IN THE TWENTY-FIRST CENTURY

O ne thing we have learned from postmodernism is that we all come at the search for truth from a particular perspective. No human perspective is value free, and no mortal is completely unbiased. That includes me. This is why it's so important that we really do have a Bible that is not merely the words of human beings but is also the Word of God. Only God can penetrate our cloud of unknowing, our cocoon of subjectivity.

This book has in some respects been hard-hitting, but I don't want it to impede the search for truth about Jesus and early Christianity. All leads should be followed and all evidence evaluated (and not ignored, much less destroyed)—the same critical scrutiny that is applied to sources like the Gnostic Gospels should be applied to the canonical material as well. Fair is fair. But when we examine all of the evidence and clues, we find that our oldest sources are still the best sources on Jesus and the history of early Christianity. Thus it is no accident that the books we find in the New Testament were canonized. Clearly, 2 Timothy 3:16, which directly applies to the Old Testament but by implication the New Testament too, is not a lie: "All scripture is inspired by God and is useful for teaching, for reproof, for correction, and for training in righteousness."

The Bible declares that history matters, that God works through historical events, that salvation was wrought by God in space and time. God rescued a real, historical Israel and sent his Son into history to redeem those who sin and fall short of the glory of God. Indeed, "our hope is based on nothing less than Jesus' blood and righteousness," not on some New Age gumbo.

Our culture has a hard time distinguishing between honesty and truth. A scholar can be completely honest and yet be dead wrong. We can be passionate about what we have learned but be misguided. A person can fall in love with a fascinating subject, giving his or her life to its study, and end up like Leigh Teabing in *The Da Vinci Code*—a deluded seeker after a Grail that is not only elusive but illusory. Don Quixote is not the only person who has tilted at windmills.

I'm afraid that this is precisely what has happened to some of the scholars who are attempting to revive ancient Gnosticism. They have been frustrated by the sins of traditional Christianity, including the arrogance and obscurantism of some Christian scholars. Looking elsewhere, they have fallen in love with the study of Gnosticism and have made the terrible mistake of selling their birthright (the canonical Gospels) for a mess of pottage (the Gnostic Gospels). This is profoundly sad.

I don't impugn the motives or the good intentions of the scholars whose work I have critiqued in this book. They work hard, and it's not a bad thing for them to be enthusiastic about their studies. Unfortunately, some of these scholars are so open-minded about the Gnostic sources that they ironically have lost their capacity to be fully critical of them. I remember the warning my grandmother gave me long ago—"Don't be so open-minded that your brains fall out." In some cases scholars have committed the very same sin they accuse evangelicals and fundamentalists of: unthinking and uncritical acceptance of dogmas—Gnostic and New Age dogma.

During the heyday of the Jesus Seminar in the 1990s, my friend and colleague Richard Hays of Duke University rightly complained about the Harvard-Claremont axis of religious influence. Scholars from these schools led us down various dead-end streets in the search for the truth of the historical Jesus. Whether it was Burton Mack's suggesting that the Gospel of Mark was a novel or even pure fiction, or J. M. Robinson's argument that there was a Q Gospel that didn't focus on the death and resurrection of Jesus, or

Helmut Koester's touting of all sorts of other documents that he called Gospels, these scholars and others like them have trained most of those who are trumpeting New Age Gnosticism as if it were a good thing. These scholars say or imply that the canon misfired. They pride themselves on their open-mindedness, but ironically they often seem to be tolerant of anything except orthodox Christianity.

To the ancients, the term *euangelion* meant "good news" (or "gospel") about something that someone—an emperor or benefactor—had done for them, some sort of undeserved but gracious action. The Gnostic Gospels, which merely offer esoteric speculations and myths, are not properly grounded in history and therefore are not good news at all. They announce the belief that self-knowledge can save us. They teach another form of self-adulation, self-worship and narcissism.

My old professor C. K. Barrett wisely said self-knowledge is not the goal of true religion, for in the end we are *not* ourselves, we have fallen and can't get up without the aid of a Redeemer who comes to us from outside ourselves. It's no good to celebrate ourselves and our self-understanding when we are not all that we were intended to be. Of course, it hurts our pride to be told that we have sinned and can't save ourselves, but "Pride goes before destruction, and a haughty spirit before a fall" (Proverbs 16:18).

Ultimately, narcissism is the sin of malignant self-love. G. K. Chesterton was right when he said that while we are in one sense to love ourselves, we should not fall in love with ourselves. If we do, it will be a monotonous courtship! When we seek the god within, whether dressed up as the "sacred feminine" or the "sacred masculine," we have committed the error of idolatry. And this is what the Gnostic documents are calling us to do. The *Gospel of Thomas* says: "If you bring forth what is within you, what you bring forth will save you. If you don't bring forth what is within you, what you do not bring forth will destroy you" (saying 45.30-33). The call to the divinity or divine spark within is not the call of the gospel of Jesus Christ. I once had a history teacher who sagaciously warned that before we replace the tried-and-true dictums of the past, we had better look very carefully at what we are putting in their place. Will we heed her advice?

If there is no ultimate authority when it comes to truth, then people are free to make their own truth. This is, in the end, what the old Gnostics did long ago, and history is repeating itself. It seems clear to me that this is what has happened to some of these scholars. Because they relativize the Bible's authority, they have no problem with putting their own ideas in its place. We are witnessing the oldest kind of intellectual sin being recommitted in the newest kinds of ways.

These scholars, though bright and sincere, are not merely wrong; they are misled. They are oblivious to the fact that they are being led down this path by the powers of darkness. The new Gnostics are too sophisticated to believe in supernatural evil, and it allows them to be misled in various unfruitful directions. C. S. Lewis once said that the devil's most successful smokescreen is to convince intelligent people that he no longer exists—they are just too smart to believe in such a being. The old Gnostics at least believed in the reality of the powers of spiritual darkness and were trying to get away from them. I wish the new Gnostics were a bit more like the old Gnostics in this respect. Then they might be more wary of the spiritual swamp into which they are wading.

Seeking the truth is good, but finding it is better. Being found by the Truth is best of all. In fact, in the person of Jesus truth has broken into space and time, and we find truth nowhere else. The truth is that God has indeed provided a record of the divine mind and plan for humankind—it's called the Bible. The Word made flesh and the written Word break through the impasse of sin and ignorance.

John 3:16 says it all—"God so loved the world that he gave his only Son, so that everyone who believes in him may not perish but may have eternal life." Notice this text doesn't say that God merely loves the intelligent, nor does it suggest that God puts a limit on who can be saved. Eternal life is open to all who place their trust in the way, the truth and the life—his Son. This is a message—the truth once given—worth shouting from the mountain tops. Gnosticism or any other form of self-help religion can't hold a candle to this mighty Light.

Finally, I want to assure women that the New Testament documents are far more affirming of women and their roles in the church and society than most of the Gnostic documents. As even Elaine Pagels has pointed out in *The Gnostic Gospels*, books such as *The Book of Thomas the Contender, The Paraphrase of Shem* and others are as misogynistic as one could imagine. In fact in the *Dialogue of the Savior* Jesus warns the disciples to pray in a place where there are no women, and "destroy the works of femaleness" (144:16-20). Women looking for affirmation of the call of God on their life won't find it in the Gnostic documents. These documents often reflect patriarchal religion and asceticism at its worst. By and large the New Testament treatment of women and their roles is a breath of fresh air when compared to the Gnostic documents.

I conclude this book with a poem I wrote a couple of Christmases ago:

THE BONDING

A cold and listless season
And full of cheerless cheer,
When hopes are raised and dashed again
And joy dissolves in tears.

The search for endless family
The search for one true Friend
Leaves questers tired, disconsolate
With questions without end.

Best find some potent pleasure quick
Some superficial thrill
Than search for everlasting love
When none can fill that bill.

So hide yourselves in shopping,
And eat until you burst,
Use endless entertainment
As shelter from the worst.

And hope at least for truce on earth,
Though warlords rattle swords
As if to kill could solve our ills
We seize our "just" rewards.

Mistake some rest for lasting peace
And calm for "all is well"
And absence of activity
As year end's victory bell.

But what if Advent is no quest
Despite the wise men's star.
What if Advent isn't reached
By driving from afar?

What if Good News comes to us
From well beyond our reach?
What if love and peace on earth
Are more than things we preach?

What if a restless peace
Is what he did intend
Until we open up our lives
And let the Stranger in?

What if a peaceless rest
Is not the Christmas hope?
What if it's nothing we could do
That helps us truly cope?

What if there is a bonding
With One who rules above
Who came to us in beggar's rags
And brought the gift of love?

The God-shaped hole in every heart
Is healed by just one source,
When Jesus comes to claim his own
Who are without recourse.

So give up endless seeking;
Surrender is required.
The One who is the Lord of all
Cannot be bought or hired.

He's not conjured into life
By pomp and circumstance,
By Yuletide carols boldly sung,
By fun or hopeful glance.

He comes unbidden, unawares,
Fills crevices of soul.
He comes on his own timely terms
And makes the sinner whole.

We shall be restless, said the saint,
Until we rest in Thee
And find that we have been reborn
Our own nativity.

How silently, how silently
The precious Truth is given.
And God imparts to human hearts
The blessings of his heaven.

(12/20/2002)

GLOSSARY

Many of the definitions in this glossary are adapted from *Pocket Dictionary of Theological Terms*, *Pocket Dictionary of Biblical Studies*, and *Pocket Dictionary for the Study of New Testament Greek* (IVP).

adoptionism. The theory that asserts that God adopted Jesus of Nazareth as his Son. In other words, Jesus was born human but became God's Son at a particular point in his life. This theory fails to reflect scriptural texts that point to Jesus' eternal relationship with the Father (e.g., John 17:5).

anthropology. The study of the status, habits, customs, relationships and culture of humankind.

anthropomorphism. A figure of speech used by writers of Scripture in which human physical characteristics are attributed to God for the sake of illustrating an important point. Anthropomorphisms essentially help to make an otherwise abstract truth about God more concrete.

apocalyptic. A term used to describe a literary genre and worldview where "secrets" are revealed about the heavenly world or the kingdom of God (and the end of the world). These secrets are usually delivered through dreams or visions or by otherworldly messengers (e.g., angels) and are expressed in vivid symbols or metaphors. Apocalyptic works flourished during the Greco-Roman period (c. 200 B.C. to A.D. 200) and are not limited to biblical books but were part of the broader culture of the Mediterranean world.

apostolicity. The correspondence of the faith and practice of the church to the authoritative New Testament teaching attributed to the apostles.

ascetic. A person who practices asceticism.

asceticism. The teaching that spirituality is attained through renunciations of physical pleasures and personal desires while concentrating on "spiritual" matters. Asceticism often assumes that the physical body is evil and is ultimately the cause of sin—a wholly unbiblical concept.

benefaction. To give aid.

benefactor. A person who gives aid to another or others.

canon. Literally meaning "standard" or "rule," the term is most closely associated with the collection of books that the church has recognized as the written Word of God (Scripture) and that functions as the rule or standard of faith and practice in the church.

canonical. Writings that are part of the biblical canon.

Christology. The theological study devoted to answering two main questions: Who is Jesus? (the question of his identity) and What is the nature and significance of what Jesus accomplished in the incarnation? (the question of his work).

codex (pl. codices). An ancient type of book produced by folding a stack of papyrus sheets or vellum (prepared animal skins) in half, then sewing the folded end to form a spine. Near the end of the first century A.D. the codex first appeared and eventually replaced the scroll as the book from of choice.

colophon. A note at the end of a book giving facts about its publication, such as the date or place of writing, or about the scribe's own personal involvement in producing it.

Dead Sea Scrolls. The collection of approximately 850 Jewish manuscripts (mostly fragmentary) discovered by shepherds in 1947 in caves near the shore of the Dead Sea. These scrolls represent all the Old Testament texts except Esther, as well as many nonbiblical texts, including commentaries and paraphrases of Old Testament books, and liturgical and eschatological works.

Didache, The. An anonymous manual of church instruction (also known as *The Teaching of the Twelve Apostles*), believed to have been written sometime between A.D. 85-150, possibly in ancient Syria. It is a unique collection of early Christian sayings and liturgical instructions on worship, baptism, the Eucharist and church leadership.

divinize. To make divine.

eschatology. Popularly known as the study of end times, eschatology seeks to understand the ultimate direction or purpose of history as it moves toward the future, both from an individual perspective (What happens when a person dies?) and from a corporate perspective (Where is history going, and how will it end?).

esoteric. Mysterious truths that are offered to and known by a select group of people.

Evangelist. In Gospel studies, one of the writers of the biblical Gospels.

exegete. A scholars who analyze passages carefully so that the words and intent of the passage are as clear as possible.

First Evangelist. The author of the Gospel of Matthew.

First Gospel. The Gospel of Matthew.

Fourth Evangelist. The author of the Gospel of John.

Fourth Gospel. The Gospel of John.

Gnosticism, Gnostics. An early Greek religious movement that was particularly influential in the second-century church. The word *gnosticism* comes from the Greek term *gnōsis*, meaning "knowledge." Gnostics believed that devotees had gained a special kind of spiritual enlightenment, through which they had attained a secret or higher level of knowledge not accessible to the uninitiated. Gnostics also tended to emphasize the spiritual realm over the material, often claiming that the material realm is evil and hence to be escaped.

heresy. Any teaching rejected by the Christian community as contrary to Scripture and hence to orthodox doctrine. Most of the teachings that have been declared heretical have to do with either the nature of God or the person of Jesus Christ. The term *heresy* is not generally used to characterize non-Christian belief.

impassible. The state of being unaffected by earthly, temporal circumstances, particularly the experience of suffering and its effects.

imprimatur. Official approval.

Johannine corpus. The books of the New Testament traditionally attributed to the author of the Gospel of John (that is, the Gospel of John, the Epistles of John and the book of Revelation).

L. Gospel material that is uniquely found in Luke's Gospel.

M. Gospel material that is uniquely found in Matthew's Gospel.

monarchianism. A movement in the second and third centuries A.D. that attempted to safeguard monotheism and the unity of the Godhead. By denying the personal reality of the Son and Spirit as separate from the Father, however, this defensive attempt resulted in an antitrinitarian heresy. Two forms of monarchianism developed: adoptionism, which understood Jesus as merely a prophet filled with the Spirit and thus "adopted" by God; and modalism, which viewed Jesus as one of the modes through which the one God reveals himself to us.

orthodox, orthodoxy. Literally, "right praise" or "right belief" (as opposed to heresy). Being orthodox implies being characterized by consistency in belief and worship with the Christian faith as witnessed to in Scripture, the early Christian writers and the official teachings, creeds and liturgy of the church. (*Orthodoxy* is also used in a narrower sense to refer to the Eastern Orthodox tradition.)

pantheism. Greek for "everything is God," the belief that God and the universe are essentially identical. More specifically, *pantheism* is the designation for the understanding of the close connection between the world and the divine reality.

papyrus. A tall, aquatic reed that grows in the Nile Delta of Egypt and was made into a writing material of the same name. Papyrus was the main writing surface throughout the Mediterranean world from the fourth century B.C. to the seventh century A.D. The earliest NT Greek manuscripts were written on papyrus.

parousia. A Greek word used to refer to the second coming of Jesus Christ at the end of history. Literally, the term means "presence." Hence it designates Christ's return as the point at which he will be fully present to the world or his presence will be fully revealed.

Passion narrative. The Gospel accounts of the events surrounding Jesus' suffering and death (that is, "passion"). The Passion narrative begins with the Jewish plot against Jesus' life during the Feast of Unleavened Bread and ends with his burial (Matthew 26–27; Mark 14–15; Luke 22–23).

Platonism. The philosophical system of the Greek philosopher Plato, who taught that anything created is an imperfect copy of a transcendent and eternal form. Human knowledge is innate and can be attained by rational reflection. Thus truth is found in the world of ideas rather than in mundane, earthly things. At death the body releases the imprisoned soul, which is then able to contemplate truth in its purest form.

provenance. Place of origin. Determining the provenance of the New Testament writings is done by evaluating internal and external evidence (early church writings and datable historical events).

Q. A hypothetical document consisting of a collection of Jesus' sayings. Q is an abbreviation of the German word *Quelle,* "source." Q accounts for sayings of Jesus that are common to the Gospels of Matthew and Luke but are not found in Mark (approximately 230 verses). Q helps to explain strong verbal agreement between Matthew and Luke. There is no universal scholarly agreement on Q's origin, date, provenance or theological perspective.

recension. A revision of an earlier text or document. The term is used especially in Old Testament and New Testament textual criticism but occasionally by literary critics to speak of stages in the transmission of a text. Technically speaking, all manuscripts are recensions of the original writings.

redemption. The process by with sinful humans are "bought back" from the bondage of sin into relationship with God through grace by the "payment" of Jesus' death.

salvation. A broad term referring to God's activity on behalf of creation and especially humans in bringing all things to God's intended goal. More specifically, salvation entails God's deliverance of humans from the power and effects of sin and the Fall through the work of Jesus Christ so that creation in general and humans in particular can enjoy the fullness of life intended for what God has made.

Second Evangelist. The author of the Gospel of Mark.

Second Gospel. The Gospel of Mark.

subordinationism. A second- and third-century heresy that held that because the Son and the Spirit proceed from the Father, they are not equal to the Father and thus not fully divine.

Synoptic Gospels. Matthew, Mark and Luke, so named because they narrate a large number of the same stories (often with word for word agreement) in the same general order, and thus they "see together" (the meaning of *synoptic*) the story of Jesus.

Synoptic Problem. The "problem" of how to account for the similarities and differences that exist among the three Synoptic Gospels. Most scholars today believe that Mark was the first Gospel to be written and that Matthew and Luke used Mark as a source, along with a sayings source identified as Q.

text(ual) criticism. The scholarly discipline of establishing the text as near to the original as possible or probable (also known as lower criticism). Since we no longer have any original manuscripts, or "autographs," scholars must sort and evaluate the extant copies with their variant wordings.

Third Evangelist. The author of the Gospel of Luke.

Third Gospel. The Gospel of Luke.

Twelve, the. The twelve male disciples that were called and named apostles
by Jesus (see Mark 3:13-19).

NOTES

The notes below are referenced by page numbers followed by brief excerpts from the pages in question to aid readers in locating the texts commented on.

Chapter 1: A Novel Idea?

Page 20: *There was a long tradition:* See for example the famous El Greco painting of the Last Supper (1570-1575) hanging in Bologna: the Beloved Disciple has fair skin and long, red hair. And there is another tradition as well that depicts Judas as having red hair and fair skin, an attribute sometimes seen as devilish (see Hans Holbein's painting of the Last Supper (1520-1524) hanging in Basel. There are then two artistic traditions of explanation for the fair-skinned, redheaded figure in the Last Supper paintings of the period of da Vinci, and neither one of them suggest a reference to Mary Magdalene. We see the tradition of the Beloved Disciple being depicted as a fair-skinned redhead already in Fra Angelico's fresco of 1438-1442 and his painting of 1450, both of which hang in Florence. This latter is a painting da Vinci could have seen. See the wonderful collection of Last Supper paintings simply titled *Last Supper* (London: Phaidon Press, 2000).

Page 23: *the witness of the Muratorian Canon:* Even earlier in the second century Marcion recognized only the Gospel of Luke as an appropriate source for knowledge about the historical Jesus.

Page 24: *"And the companion of the":* Quotations from the *Gospel of Philip* are taken from *The Nag Hammadi Library in English*, ed. James M. Robinson, 3rd ed. (San Francisco: Harper & Row, 1988).

Page 24: *But as Karen King says:* Karen L. King, *The Gospel of Mary of Magdala* (Santa Rosa, Calif.: Polebridge, 2003).

Page 24: *there were already exceptions to this sort of rule:* See, for example, Josephus *Antiquities of the Jews* 18.1.5.20-21, *Jewish Wars* 2.8.2; and Philo *Hypothetica* 11.14-17.

Chapter 2: No Weddings and a Funeral

Page 29:   *first union was still in effect:* I treat this at length in my book *Women in the Ministry of Jesus* (New York: Cambridge University Press, 1984).

Page 29:   *it's better for a man not to marry:* The exception clauses found in Matthew 5:32 and 19:9 refer to an exception for *porneia*. This term does not mean "adultery," for which there is another Greek term—*moicheia*. The root meaning of *porneia* is "prostitution," for a *pornē* was a prostitute. But the word eventually came to refer to incest and by extension all sorts of unusual and inappropriate sexual relationships. In this context Jesus may have been referring to the incestuous relationship between Herod Antipas and his brother's wife. John the Baptist, it will be remembered condemned that relationship and lost his head because of it.

Page 31:   *The case that Jesus was married:* W. E. Phipps, *Was Jesus Married?* (New York: Harper & Row, 1970).

Page 31:   *Paul assumes his audience knows:* I have written more on this issue in my book *New Testament History* (Grand Rapids: Baker, 2001).

Page 32:   *"The codices date to the 4th century":* Gary Lease and Birger Pearson, "Nag Hammadi," in *Anchor Bible Dictionary*, ed. David Noel Freedman (New York, Doubleday, 1992), 4:982.

Page 34:   *"theology is really anthropology":* Elaine Pagels, *The Gnostic Gospels* (New York: Vintage Books, 1981), p. 123.

Page 34:   *But Andrew answered and said:* The translation of the *Gospel of Mary* here is from *The Nag Hammadi Library in English*, ed. James M. Robinson, 3rd ed. (San Francisco: Harper & Row, 1988).

Page 35:   *Tell me, what do you think of these things she has been telling us?:* Here I am following Jean-Yves Leloup's translation *The Gospel of Mary Magdalene* (Rochester, Vt.: Inner Traditions, 2002), p. 17, lines 10-13 of the Coptic manuscript (emphasis added).

Page 36:   *as Jean-Yves Leloup insists on translating:* Leloup, *Gospel of Mary Magdalene*, p. 9, line 18.

Page 36:   *She is not Wisdom:* See Karen L. King, *The Gospel of Mary of Magdala* (Santa Rosa, Calif.: Polebridge, 2003), pp. 146-48.

Chapter 3: Tell Me the Old, Old Story

Page 38:   *the New Testament offers a very high view of women:* See, for example, my book *Women and the Genesis of Christianity* (New York: Cambridge University Press, 1990).

Page 38: *The term* gospel *comes to us:* For more detail on what follows see my introduction to the New Testament, *The New Testament Story* (Grand Rapids: Eerdmans, 2004).

Page 39: *the early Christian document called the* Didache: See *Didache* 8.2; 11.3; 15.3-4.

Page 40: *Apart from the Passion narrative:* For more on what follows, see my book *The Gospel of Mark: A Socio-Rhetorical Commentary* (Grand Rapids: Eerdmans, 2001).

Page 41: *the right length to fit on an ancient scroll:* Mark has 11,242 words, Matthew has 18,305 words, and John has 16,150 words. The longest of all the Gospels is Luke's, which with 19,428 words puts it right at the upper limits of what a scroll could hold.

Page 45: *Jesus as both a sage and as the embodiment of Wisdom:* I take up this idea in detail in my book *Jesus the Sage* (Minneapolis: Fortress, 1994).

Page 46: *His work also follows the convention:* I say more about this in my book *The Acts of the Apostles* (Grand Rapids, Mich.: Eerdmans, 1998).

Page 48: *As different as the Gospel of John is:* I take this up in detail in my book *John's Wisdom* (Louisville, Ky.: Westminster John Knox, 1995).

Chapter 4: His Story, History and the Canon's Story

Page 53: *Inquiring minds need to know:* Some of what follows in the next few pages is found in a different form in my *The Many Faces of the Christ* (New York: Crossroad, 1998).

Page 54: *Irenaeus learned from and echoes Justin Martyr:* See S. Duffy, "The Early Church Fathers and the Great Councils: The Emergence of Classical Christianity," in *Jesus: One and Many,* ed. E. Richard (Wilmington, Del.: Glazier, 1988), p. 444.

Page 55: *Tertullian helped to shape the later councils' discussion:* See *Against Praxeas.* Tertullian, however, spoke of one *persona* with two *substantiae,* namely, flesh and spirit. See Duffy, "Early Church Fathers," pp. 447-48.

Page 58: *This is not to say that there weren't residual concerns:* Some church fathers saw *homoousios* as a convenient translation of Tertullian's earlier phrase *unius substantiae* ("one substance"). But others worried this negated the three persons, or the three *hypostaseis,* of the Godhead. The unforeseen problem was that *hypostaseis* was a proper Greek translation for the Latin term *substantiae.* Therefore, when some Greek-speaking Christians heard the arguments that the Father and the Son were *unius* substantiae, they assumed this meant one *hypostasis*, which was not Tertullian's or Nicaea's view.

Page 58:   *"Of the wise among ourselves"*: Gregory of Nazianzus *Theological Oration 5 (Oration 32) 5.*

Page 58:   *Two of the key figures who helped resolve the issue*: Athanasius discusses the Holy Spirit in four letters to Serapion. Basil's thought is contained in his great treatise "On the Holy Spirit."

Page 60:   *God "feels bodily pain"*: See the helpful discussion of all these matters in Jaroslav Pelikan, *The Christian Tradition* (Chicago: University of Chicago Press, 1971), 1:172-77; and also J. N. D. Kelly, *Early Christian Doctrines* (New York: Harper & Row, 1958), pp. 56-60, 83-162.

Page 61:   *Following therefore the holy Fathers*: The Chalcedonian definition is available in several English translations. This is my own slightly modernized version.

Page 61:   *I have provided only a small portion*: I have skipped, for instance, the council that was held in A.D. 381 at Constantinople (between Nicaea and Chalcedon). There the views of Apollinarius were condemned, safeguarding Christ's humanity.

Page 61:   *the discussion went beyond the New Testament data*: In certain cases some Christians would say the councils' discussions went *against* the New Testament data. For instance, the Greek notions of the impassibility and unchangeableness of God causes severe problems for the doctrine of the incarnation. Surely Christ's taking on a human nature constitutes a change in the Godhead.

Page 62:   *Development of Canon and Christology*: The Nicene Creed issued from the Council in A.D. 325 is considerably shorter than the version commonly used in Christian worship today. The longer version is more formally known as the Niceno-Constantinopolitan Creed.

Page 63:   *Constantine ruled as Roman Emperor*: The extent of Constantine's reign depends on whether we date his rule from the time his troops proclaimed him emperor or some later date.

Page 63:   *Constantine himself became a Christian*: It is notable that he was only baptized shortly before his death, but then many Christians of that era seem to have followed that practice, fearful they would be lost if they committed any postbaptismal sins.

Page 65:   *What Eusebius's* Life of Constantine *does say*: See Eusebius *Life of Constantine* book 4, chapter 36.

Page 65:   *Eusebius also says that Constantine:* Eusebius *Life of Constantine* book
            3, chapter 64.

Chapter 5: Something About Mary

Page 70:   *extravagant claims made about Mary Magdalene:* Some of this material
            appears in my "Mary, Mary Extraordinary," Beliefnet.com, October 29,
            2003 <beliefnet.com/story/135/story_13503_1.html>.

Page 72:   *criticized for being an exorcist:* The most frequently mentioned miracle
            that Jesus performs in our earliest Gospel, Mark, is exorcism, and Luke
            as well speaks of such miracles. It is interesting that our latest Gospel,
            John, entirely omits any references to Jesus being an exorcist. This is
            surely because this was one of the most controversial aspects of his heal-
            ing ministry, and it led to the charge that he was in league with Satan
            (see Mark 3).

Page 72:   *We cannot be sure of this:* It would be a mistake to assume that the
            women listed in Luke 8:1-3 were just the "hospitality brigade" for the
            men. But even if we emphasize the provisioning side of the equation, it
            still tells us that some of these women, perhaps especially Joanna, were
            women of means. Luke 8:1-3 shows how all persons, including the least,
            the last and the lost were accepted by Jesus as traveling disciples. And it
            specially focuses on women, such as Mary Magdalene, that Jesus
            helped or healed.

Page 73:   *they were there till the bitter end:* When watchmen were not placed on
            the site where executions took place, some criminals were surrepti-
            tiously taken down from crosses. Presumably these women were not
            considered a threat to do so.

Page 74:   *Mark 16:9-20 is missing from all the earliest and best manuscripts:* These
            verses were added sometime in the second century because the Gospel
            was felt to be incomplete if it ended at Mark 16:8, especially with the fi-
            nal phrase being "for they were afraid."

Page 74:   *two Marys discovered the empty tomb:* See my *John's Wisdom* (Louis-
            ville, Ky.: Westminster John Knox, 1995) for a more fully developed dis-
            cussion of the issues I am summarizing here.

Page 76:   *the impact of the risen Jesus:* For a magisterial treatment of the resurrec-
            tion, you may want to read N. T. Wright's *The Resurrection of the Son of
            God* (Minneapolis: Fortress, 2003).

Page 77:   *the way he rebukes Mary here:* It is important however not to overdo the contrast between Mary Magdalene and Thomas. Thomas's unbelief is more severe than Mary's, and he persists in it even after the reports that Jesus is risen. Since Jesus appeared to Mary first, she only had a pre-Easter knowledge of Jesus to guide her response. Thomas's spiritual obtuseness is portrayed as more reprehensible. Mary, having once touched Jesus, does not need to cling to him, but rather can be commissioned to undertake an apostolic task—proclaiming the good news of the risen Jesus to the others. In other words, Mary comes off better in this story than Thomas or even Peter and the Beloved Disciple for that matter.

Chapter 6: Those in the Know

Page 84:   *We can say this with some assurance*: Of course we know that Plato's *Republic*, the *Sentences* of Sextus and one other document in the Nag Hammadi library are from an earlier period.

Page 85:   *Seth is also portrayed as a revealer figure*: Sethian literature includes the *Apocryphon of John*, the *Hypostasis of Archons*, the *Gospel of the Egyptians*, the *Apocalypse of Adam*, the *Three Steles of Seth, Zostrianos, Melchizedek*, the *Thought of Norea, Marsanes, Allogenes* and *Trimorphic Protennoia*.

Page 85:   *before Gnosticism was officially repudiated*: Birger A. Pearson discusses this more fully in "Nag Hammadi: Codices," in the *Anchor Bible Dictionary*, ed. David Noel Freedman (New York, Doubleday, 1992), 4:984-93.

Page 86:   *Some said, "Mary conceived by the holy spirit"*: The translations of the *Gospel of Philip* come from the standard work *The Nag Hammadi Library in English*, ed. James M. Robinson, 3rd ed. (San Francisco: Harper & Row, 1988). The Scripture references within parentheses have been added to the text by the translator to aid readers in identifying quotations from or allusions to the canonical Scriptures.

Page 89:   *composed toward the end of the second century* A.D.: Pheme Perkins, "Mary, Gospel of," *Anchor Bible Dictionary*, ed. David Noel Freedman (New York: Doubleday, 1992), 4:583-84.

Page 90:   *not to participate in physical passions*: *Gospel of Mary* 7, 1–8, 10.

Page 90:   *made into a man*: Lest we think these texts are somehow feminist texts, the phrase "made into men" reminds us that this is not so. However, there may be an assumption that men have more difficulty in struggling with physical passions, and so women can sometimes be better examples of being the true ascetic and so the true Gnostic.

Page 90: *the soul ascends past the cosmic powers: Gospel of Mary* 15,1–17,9.

Page 91: *the martyrdom of Perpetua:* Perpetua died in A.D. 203 under the reign of Septimus Severus, when there was a great persecution (A.D. 193-211). See "The Acts of Perpetua and Felicitas."

Page 93: *The problem wasn't the insistence:* Frederica Mathewes-Green, "What Heresy?" *Books & Culture* (November-December 2003).

Page 93: *Matter is real:* Eugene Peterson, *The Contemplative Pastor: Returning to the Art of Spiritual Direction* (Grand Rapids, Mich.: Eerdmans, 1993), p. 68.

Chapter 7: Doubting Thomas

Page 100: *Jesus said to them:* In this chapter for the *Gospel of Thomas*, I am generally following the translation in Elaine Pagels's *Beyond Belief* (New York: Random House, 2003), pp. 227-42.

Page 100: *As Pagels herself points out:* One of the purposes of Pagels's new book is to argue that the *Gospel of Thomas* is a source for some of the material in the Gospel of John (see *Beyond Belief,* pp. 50-75). Not many Johannine scholars will be convinced of this, not least because of the different theological orientation the two books have. Some see it as just another unsuccessful attempt to date *Thomas* early, implying that it comes from the New Testament era. This ignores the evidence amassed by various scholars that shows *Thomas* reflects a knowledge of all the canonical Gospels, including of their editing tendencies and special material.

Page 102: *Most of this Gospel is only available in Coptic:* The Coptic version of the *Gospel of Thomas* survives in Codex II of the Nag Hammadi library; portions of the Greek version survive in *Oxyrhynchus Papyri* 1,654 and 655.

Page 102: *Most scholars think the original document:* See for example Craig A. Evans, "Thomas, the Gospel of," in *Dictionary of the Later New Testament and Its Developments,* ed. Ralph P. Martin and Peter H. Davids (Downers Grove, Ill.: InterVarsity Press, 1997), pp. 1175-77.

Page 102: *edited in a more Gnostic direction:* On all of this, see my *Jesus the Sage* (Minneapolis: Fortress, 1994), pp. 211-19.

Page 102: *Greek text dates to about A.D. 200: Oxyrhynchus Papyrus* 1 dates to about A.D. 200. It is the earliest Greek portion of the *Gospel of Thomas* because the other Greek portion, *Oxyrhynchus Papyri* 654 and 655, dates to the middle of the third century. One thing that helps us to date this document is the fact that Hippolytus quotes logion (saying) 4 and mentions its title in the first third of the third century.

Page 102:   *Matthew's form of Q:* P. J. Hartin, *James and the Q Sayings of Jesus* (Sheffield, England: JSOT Press, 1991), pp. 57-58. Depending on when we date James (in my view it was written by the brother of Jesus in the 50s), it provides an independent witness in addition to the Q material that the teachings of Jesus early on did not have either the Gnostic or ascetical bent that we find in the *Thomas* versions of Jesus' teachings.

Page 103:   *Klyne Snodgrass and C. M. Tuckett:* There isn't room for a detailed demonstration of this fact here, so see Klyne Snodgrass, "The Gospel of Thomas: A Secondary Gospel," *Second Century* 7 (1989-1990): 19-38, and C. M. Tuckett, "Thomas and the Synoptics," *Novum Testamentum* 30 (1988): 132-57.

Page 103:   *As Craig Evans says:* See Evans, "Thomas, the Gospel of," p. 1176.

Page 103:   *The* Gospel of Thomas *also reflects:* See Craig A. Evans, "Jesus in the Agrapha and Apocryphal Gospels," in *Studying the Historical Jesus,* ed. Bruce Chilton and Craig A. Evans (New York: Brill 1994), pp. 479-533.

Page 103:   *James D. G. Dunn draws this conclusion:* James D. G. Dunn, *The Evidence for Jesus* (Philadelphia: Westminster Press, 1985), p. 98.

Page 104:   Thomas *sometimes gives us an earlier version:* Saying 65 about the vineyard may be one example of an earlier version of an authentic saying of Jesus.

Page 105:   *women teachers in Gnostic circles:* See Tertullian *Prescription Versus Heretics* 41.

Page 105:   *Now you can begin to see:* Frederica Mathewes-Green, "What Heresy?" *Books & Culture,* November-December 2003, pp. 23, 22.

Page 105:   *neither Jew nor Greek:* It is instructive to keep in mind the Gnostic notion found in some documents that the original human may have been androgynous and in the end male and female needed to reunite into one person—perhaps identical with the Perfect Man.

Page 106:   *a kind of historical amnesia:* Philip Jenkins, *Hidden Gospels: How the Search for Jesus Lost Its Way* (New York: Oxford University Press, 2001), pp. 208, 216.

Page 107:   *"remained multiform":* Elaine Pagels, *The Gnostic Gospels* (New York: Vintage Books, 1981), p. 142.

Page 107:   *This is a false vision:* See Pagels's comments on this in *Gnostic Gospels*, p. 151.

Page 107:   *diversity of first-century Christianity:* See Dunn's discussion in *Evidence for Jesus*, pp. 96-99.

Page 108:   *It adds precious little to our knowledge of the historical Jesus:* In some Valentinian Gnostic texts there is reference to a divine Mother as well as a divine Father (see Pagels, *Gnostic Gospels*, pp. 48-69). This probably shouldn't be seen as evidence for pagan goddess worship within the ascetic Gnostic sect. Those pagan goddesses certainly weren't symbols of asceticism, rather they were fertility goddesses, which would be abhorrent to the Gnostics. What seems to be going on in the Gnostic texts, though it is always hard to be sure, is that just as the Gnostics had a theology of a primordial person who was male-female, they assumed that the divine too was male-female. Thus the modern attempt to blend goddess worship with Gnostic elements needs to be seen as a modern form of syncretism that probably has no roots in ancient Gnosticism. In other words, Dan Brown's *The Da Vinci Code* is confused on this score, as are other modern advocates of New Age Gnosticism.

Page 108:   *John's message contrasts:* Pagels, *Beyond Belief*, p. 68.

Chapter 8: Consulting the Canon Professors

Page 113:   *We now begin to see:* Elaine Pagels, *The Gnostic Gospels* (New York: Vintage Books, 1981), p. xxxv.

Page 115:   *Gnostic exegetes were only interested:* See Pheme Perkins, "Gnosticism and the Christian Bible," in *The Canon Debate*, ed. Lee Martin McDonald and James A. Sanders (Peabody, Mass.: Hendrickson, 2002), p. 371.

Page 118:   *These writings are of inestimable importance:* Karen L. King, *The Gospel of Mary of Magdala* (Santa Rosa, Calif.: Polebridge, 2003), p. 157.

Page 119:   *"emulate their struggles to make Christianity":* King, *Gospel of Mary of Magdala*, p. 158.

Page 119:   *According to King:* King, *Gospel of Mary of Magdala*, p. 161.

Page 120:   *The raw stuff, the beginning articulation:* See my discussion in *The Many Faces of Christ* (New York: Crossroad, 1996), pp. 225-31.

Page 121:   *conclusions of the text critics:* It's not possible to review in detail the criteria used to reconstruct the earliest form of a New Testament text, but here are a few basic principles of text criticism: (1) Earlier manuscripts should be given priority. (2) Readings that best explain differing readings in subsequent copies of a manuscript are to be preferred. (3) Sometimes the more difficult reading is likely to be closer to the original since scribes tended to smooth out textual infelicities. (4) Manuscripts must be weighed and not just counted. The fact that a particular reading in a verse has the support of the majority of manuscripts does not mean it is original. The quality of a manuscript tradition and not just the quantity of support must be considered.

Page 122:   In a helpful article G. N. Stanton has shown: "The Earliest Reception of Matthew's Gospel," in The Gospel of Matthew in Current Study, ed. David E. Aune (Grand Rapids: Eerdmans, 2001), pp. 42-61, here pp. 50-51.

Page 123:   ad hominem arguments go too far: See Bart D. Ehrman, Orthodox Corruption of Scripture (New York: Oxford University Press, 1997), pp. 18-31. One of the more disturbing parts of Ehrman's discussion is his insinuation that the orthodox corruptions of the text are little different from the way the text today is twisted today to serve the purposes of certain groups and individuals (pp. 30-31). Truth is, despite his disclaimers at junctures, he is accusing various church fathers of lying, bad faith and, in the case of various orthodox scribes, forgery. He does not sufficiently counterbalance that discussion with the many persons of integrity, such as Bishop Serapion. It is clear enough that Ehrman takes a very postmodern approach to "meaning" and the active role of the reader in construing the text. For him, meaning is in the eye of the beholder, it would seem. Of course this would also include Ehrman. It is clear enough that he has an agenda in the way he reads the textual data. He "exposes" the chicanery of early orthodox scribes and suggests that orthodoxy was built on such duplicitous practices even though he suggests they were often oblivious to what they were doing. Ehrman's error is clearly a historicism hostile to theology.

Page 123:   established long before the Council of Nicaea: To give but one telling illustration of why it was so clear to the church fathers that the Gnostics were in error and guilty of distorting the history of early Christianity compare the canonical Gospel portraits of Jesus' Passion with the Apocalypse of Peter, which depicts Jesus laughing on the cross as if he were a radiant being of Gnostic light! (81,10-11). It is not true that the Gnostics were first denounced in the fourth century, for they were already denounced by the church fathers in the second century.

Page 123: *he stopped its use:* See Ehrman, *Orthodox Corruption of Scripture,* p. 18.

Page 124: *From the outset Hengel stresses:* Martin Hengel, *The Four Gospels and the One Gospel of Jesus Christ,* trans. John Bowden (Harrisburg, Penn.: Trinity Press, 2000), p. 9.

Page 125: *didn't impose their views:* What finally assured the acceptance of the book of Hebrews was its incorporation into the collection of Pauline letters. This seems to have happened in Alexandria around A.D. 170. See L. M. McDonald, "Canon," in *Dictionary of the Later New Testament and Its Developments,* ed. Ralph P. Martin and Peter H. Davids (Downers Grove, Ill.: InterVarsity Press, 1997), p. 138. One of the more significant points is that probably from the third century onward many churches already had a core New Testament collection that included the four canonical Gospels, Acts, thirteen Pauline Epistles, 1 Peter and 1 John, though there was no unanimity (see *Canon Debate,* ed. Lee McDonald and James A. Sanders [Peabody: Hendrickson, 2002], p. 415).

Page 125: *The final stages of the closing:* McDonald, "Canon," p. 134.

Page 127: *The gospel about Jesus:* James D. G. Dunn, "Has the Canon a Continuing Function?" in *The Canon Debate,* ed. Lee Martin McDonald and James A. Sanders (Peabody, Mass.: Hendrickson, 2002), pp. 567-68.

Page 128: *Dunn says, "If the conviction":* Dunn, "Has the Canon a Continuing Function?" p. 578.

Page 129: *"The strength of this saying is":* Pagels, *Beyond Belief,* p. 32.

Page 130: *"I am Thou":* Pagels, *Beyond Belief,* p. 75.

Chapter 9: Reading Borg Again for the First Time

Page 134: *"Resurrection," with the various words:* N. T. Wright, *The Resurrection of the Son of God* (Minneapolis: Fortress, 2003), p. 201.

Page 135: *"This widespread belief in the future resurrection":* Wright, *Resurrection of the Son of God,* p. 203.

Page 135: *Paul's letters, the earliest treatment of the resurrection:* See Wright, *Resurrection of the Son of God,* pp. 209-398.

Page 136: *The enormous pressure in some parts:* Wright, *Resurrection of the Son of God,* pp. 433-34.

Page 137: *The "ruling hypothesis in much New Testament study":* Wright, *Resurrection of the Son of God,* p. 675.

Page 138: *What if the resurrection:* Wright, *Resurrection of the Son of God,* p. 713.

Page 139: *Presumably the emphasis falls on "experience":* Brian C. Jones's review of *Reading the Bible Again for the First Time* by Marcus Borg, Review of Biblical Literature <www.bookreviews.org/pdf/2831_2780.pdf>, p. 5.

Page 140:   *the Bible is one vehicle:* Marcus J. Borg, *Reading the Bible Again for the First Time* (San Francisco: HarperSanFrancisco, 2001), pp. 30-31.

Page 140:   *But in the end the true view of "traditional Christianity":* All quotations in this paragraph are from Borg, *Reading the Bible Again*, pp. 13-18.

Page 141:   *Such stories, he says:* Borg, *Reading the Bible Again*, p. 47.

Page 142:   *Why are historical claims so important:* Jones, review of *Reading the Bible Again for the First Time*, p. 5.

Page 143:   *As even Borg himself admits:* Borg, *Reading the Bible Again*, p. 265.

Page 144:   *The Bible doesn't tell us how it should be read:* Borg, *Reading the Bible Again*, p. 27.

Page 144:   *The Bible becomes a critical dialogue partner:* Borg, *Reading the Bible Again*, p. 30.

Page 145:   *First, the truth of the Bible:* Here I am not just speaking of how the Bible becomes the place where we can encounter God's presence, as Borg affirms, but also how God uses his Word to say something quite specific to modern persons.

Chapter 10: What If God Was One of Us?

Page 152:   *"The expression* I will be *is a historical formula":* S. R. Driver, *The Book of Exodus* (Cambridge: Cambridge University Press, 1953), pp. 40-41.

Page 153:   *The God of the Old Testament:* Some of what follows appears in another form in the book I wrote with Laura Ice titled, *The Shadow of the Almighty* (Grand Rapids,: Eerdmans, 2000).

Page 153:   *Yet as Walter Brueggemann stresses:* Walter Brueggemann, *Theology of the Old Testament* (Minneapolis: Fortress, 1997), pp. 244-47.

Page 154:   *Psalm 89:26 says:* For more on the discussion of God as Father, see Helmer Ringgren, "אָב *'ābh*," in *Theological Dictionary of the Old Testament*, ed. G. Johannes Botterweck, Helmer Ringgren, Heinz-Josef Fabry (Grand Rapids: Eerdmans, 1978), 1:16-19.

Page 155:   *adoption of Israel's king:* Marianne Meye Thompson suggests the following taxonomy of God as Father: (1) God is father in the sense of the origin of a family of people or the one who provides an inheritance to his children, (2) God is the father who provides for and protects his children, (3) obedience and honor are due to God as they are to a father. This taxonomy starts with the functions of human fathers and then predicates them of God (see *The Promise of the Father* [Louisville, Ky.: Westminster John Knox, 2000], p. 39).

Page 155: *is evident that the father:* Brueggemann, *Theology of the Old Testament,* p. 247.

Page 155: *Compared to other Near Eastern cultures of the time:* "The fundamentally new achievement of the second millennium was its genius in lighting upon a new metaphor truly suggestive of essential elements in the human response to numinous experience. This parent metaphor, which saw the Numinous as a father or a mother, significantly enhanced and deepened the sense of fascinosum that was present already in the worship of the fertility gods. . . . It enhanced and deepened it by recognizing and expressing a personal relationship to the divine, a sense of attraction being reciprocal. Man, who under the ruler metaphor was subject and slave, gained sonship" (Thorkild Jacobsen, *The Treasures of Darkness: A History of Mesopotamian Religion* [New Haven, Conn.: Yale University Press, 1976), pp. 225-26]).

Page 155: *and the New Testament:* "The relative infrequency of the term 'Father' for God does contrast sharply with the regular use of the term in the New Testament. But the scarcity of the term as over against the New Testament does not signal radical discontinuity with the presentation of God in the Old Testament" (Meye Thompson, *Promise of the Father,* p. 39).

Page 155: *Israel was surrounded by nations:* Willem A. VanGemeren, "'Abba' in the Old Testament?" *JETS* 31 (1988): 392.

Page 156: *"change . . . has less to do with matter of culture":* Christopher Seitz, *Word Without End* (Grand Rapids: Eerdmans, 1998), p. 258.

Page 157: *This may suggest a growing tendency:* See Meye Thompson, *Promise of the Father,* p. 51.

Page 157: *material in the later Jewish writings:* The texts in question are Babylonian Talmud Taanit 23b, Targum Psalm 89:27, and Targum Malachi 2:10, with the first of these being the most important.

Page 157: *Jesus' use of the Aramaic abba:* See Meye Thompson, *Promise of the Father,* p. 50.

Page 157: *Meye Thompson claims that the Jewish naming:* Meye Thompson, *Promise of the Father,* p. 54.

Page 158: *All of these factors reveal:* I would like to express appreciation for the foundational and helpful work done by Marianne Meye Thompson in

The Promise of the Father. This chapter is indebted to her work even though I have certainly differed with some of her judgments.

Page 159: *God provides some precedent for Jesus' use of father language:* For a contrary view, Meye Thompson argues that "Jesus understood God first as the father of the people of Israel, and his own relationship to God in and from that framework" (*Promise of the Father*, p. 79). She fails to grasp the radicality of Jesus' own ministry and mission. She argues that "to trust God as Father is thus not to come to a new intimacy with God but, rather, to renew one's trust in the God of Israel" (p. 84). This is simply incorrect. Jesus believed Israel was basically lost and needed to be redeemed. He, like John the Baptist, called for radical repentance and warned of judgment, which would even come on Israelites if they did not repent. The new eschatological covenant was not seen as a mere renewing of the old covenant. Repentance, discipleship and taking on the yoke of the new covenant meant coming to a new intimacy with God that allowed a person to address God as *abba*, as enabled and prompted by the eschatological Spirit, which Jesus promised.

Page 159: *"the complete novelty and uniqueness of 'Abbā":* Joachim Jeremias, *New Testament Theology* (New York: Scribner, 1971), p. 67.

Page 160: *impact of Jesus' use of* abba: This is analogous to looking at an enormous crater made by a meteor. Though there are only small traces of the meteor itself, the size of the crater clearly bears witness to the original size of the meteor. Though the evidence for Jesus' use of *abba* in the Gospels is not plentiful, nevertheless its importance can be judged by its impact on his earliest followers. Paul was one of those earliest followers, having been converted within a few years of Jesus' death.

Page 160: *the Father's active care:* Consider the noteworthy comments of feminist theologian Elizabeth A. Johnson: "From the way Jesus talked about God and enacted the reign of God, it is obvious that he had a special and original experience of God as intimate, close, and tremendously compassionate over human suffering and sin. Out of that experience Jesus surfaced a name for God, namely *Abba*. . . . Jesus' own personal experience of God as close and compassionate led him to name God in his very intimate way, *Abba*. The name evokes the power of a very close relationship between Jesus and the One he names this way. Furthermore, Jesus teaches others to call God *Abba*, encouraging them to trust God the way little children trust a good parent to take care of them, be compassionate over their weakness, and stand guard against those who would harm them. Jesus' *Abba* experience is the heart of the matter, the dynamism behind his preaching the reign of God and of his typical way of acting. God *Abba* was the passion of his life" (*Consider Jesus* [New York: Crossroad, 1990], p. 57).

Page 161:   *By the Spirit the presence of God replicates:* James D. G. Dunn, *Jesus and the Spirit* (Philadelphia: Westminster Press, 1975), pp. 317-19.

Page 161:   *Every one of the Pauline letters begins with:* For "our Father" see Romans 1:7; 1 Corinthians 1:3; 2 Corinthians 1:2; Galatians 1:3-4; Ephesians 1:2; Philippians 1:2; Colossians 1:2 for "the Father" see Galatians 1:1; 1 Thessalonians 1:1; 1 Timothy 1:2; 2 Timothy 1:2; Titus 1:4; and for "the Father of our Lord Jesus Christ" see 2 Corinthians 1:3; Ephesians 1:3; Colossians 1:3.

Page 161-62: *The story of Jesus, not the story of Israel:* For a contrary view, see Meye Thompson, *Promise of the Father*, p. 132.

Page 162:   *replicated the prayer life of the Son.* See Dunn, *Jesus and the Spirit*, pp. 317-19.

Page 162:   *There is no precedent for this:* Targum I on Leviticus 22:28 does indeed say, "My people, children of Israel, as our Father is merciful in heaven, so you shall be merciful on earth" (compare Targum on Isaiah 63:16 and 64:8). These texts however are notoriously difficult to date and probably come from after the time of Jesus, perhaps after the New Testament era. In other words, they may reflect the influence of Jesus' and early Christian teaching on Jewish teaching, which did happen in other cases, for example in speculation about the Suffering Servant of Isaiah 53.

Page 163:   *As Meye Thompson stresses:* Meye Thompson, *Promise of the Father*, p. 93.

Page 164:   *Meye Thompson compares parallel passages:* Meye Thompson, *Promise of the Father*, p. 105.

Page 164:   *S. C. Barton is surely right:* Stepehn C. Barton, *The Spirituality of the Gospels* (London: SPCK, 1992), p. 12, as cited in Meye Thompson, *Promise of the Father*, p. 106.

Page 164:   *"Matthew still retains the singularity":* Meye Thompson, *Promise of the Father*, p. 111. This is correct and precisely why citing a saying like Jeremiah 3:19 as a parallel is not very apt, for there God is hoping that all true Israelites would call him "my Father" (even though, in the event, they have not done so, but rather have been unfaithful).

Page 165:   *only begotten, or "natural," Son:* See my book *John's Wisdom* (Louisville, Ky.: Westminster John Knox, 1995), pp. 54-55.

Page 165:   *only Jesus addresses God as "Father":* There are some editorial examples of the use of *Father* such as in John 5:18, which shows that the usage also reflects what was going on in the Fourth Evangelist's day.

Page 165:   *What is particularly telling:* Meye Thompson, *Promise of the Father,* p. 134.

Page 166:   *People must first become children of God:* It is not going too far then to say that in John "There is no Father without the Son. Father is not something that God is apart from relationship to the Son" (Meye Thompson, *Promise of the Father,* p. 137).

Page 166:   *"The 'kinship' of God and Jesus":* Meye Thompson, *Promise of the Father,* p. 136.

Page 168:   *Then why is God named:* Whether one wants to call *Father* a name or a nickname, clearly it is a label used to invoke or address a particular being. There may be some analogy with the way the term *Christ* became a virtual second name for Jesus.

Page 168:   *Many within the Christian family:* Donald Juel, "The Lord's Prayer in the Gospels of Matthew and Luke," in *The Lord's Prayer: Perspectives for Reclaiming Christian Prayer,* ed. Daniel L. Migliore (Grand Rapids: Eerdmans, 1993), p. 58.

Page 169:   *viewed as an act of infidelity:* Read what Ezekiel 23 says about spiritual infidelity in Israel.

A SELECT BIBLIOGRAPHY

Books and Articles by Ben Witherington III

The Acts of the Apostles. Grand Rapids: Eerdmans, 1998. A commentary that looks at the larger issues of historical accuracy and the social and political settings in the development of the early church.

The Gospel of Mark. Grand Rapids: Eerdmans, 2001. A commentary that views the Gospel of Mark as both ancient biography and ancient rhetoric.

Jesus the Sage. Minneapolis: Fortress, 1994. A history of Wisdom in the Old and New Testaments and how it applies to Jesus as a sage and the very embodiment of Wisdom

Jesus the Seer. Peabody, Mass.: Hendrickson, 1999. A study of the broader expression of prophecy in its ancient Mediterranean context to better understand biblical prophecy, particularly about and by Jesus.

John's Wisdom. Louisville, Ky.: Westminster John Knox, 1995. A commentary on the Gospel of John that highlights its Wisdom orientation to Jesus and his teachings.

The Many Faces of Christ. New York: Crossroad, 1998. An examination of who the historical Jesus was from the perspectives of those around him. The result is not one generic Christology but many complementary Christologies.

"Mary, Mary Extraordinary." Beliefnet.com, October 29, 2003 <beliefnet.com/story/135/story_13503_1.html>. An online article that looks for historical evidence for an intimate relationship between Mary Magdalene and Jesus.

New Testament History. Grand Rapids: Baker, 2001. A narrative history of events surrounding New Testament times from the intertestamental Maccabean Wars to the reign of Domitian. It especially focuses on the life of Jesus and the development of the early church.

The New Testament Story. Grand Rapids: Eerdmans, 2004. A discussion of how the
New Testament books were produced and the story of each of the books, particularly focusing on the Gospels.

The Shadow of the Almighty. Grand Rapids: Eerdmans, 2000. An introduction to
early trinitarian thought that looks at *Father, Son,* and *Holy Spirit* in biblical perspective. Coauthored by Laura M. Ice.

Women and the Genesis of Christianity. New York: Cambridge University Press,
1990. An examination of how Jesus broke significantly with convention in his
view of women, offering a wholly new conception of the legitimate rights of
women in society.

Women in the Earliest Churches. Cambridge: Cambridge University Press, 1988. A
survey of views about women held by various New Testament people. It analyzes
the roles and functions that women assumed in the early Christian communities
from A.D. 33 to the Council of Nicaea.

Women in the Ministry of Jesus. New York: Cambridge University Press, 1984. A
study of Jesus' attitudes toward women and their roles as reflected in his earthly
life.

Recommended Reading

Bock, Darrell L. *Breaking the Da Vinci Code.* Nashville: Thomas Nelson, 2004.

Dunn, James D. G. *The Unity and Diversity of the New Testament.* Philadelphia:
Westminster John Knox Press, 1977.

Evans, Craig A. "Thomas, the Gospel of." In *Dictionary of the Later New Testament
and Its Developments.* Edited by Ralph P. Martin and Peter H. Davids. Downers
Grove, Ill.: InterVarsity Press, 1997.

Hengel, Martin. *The Four Gospels and the One Gospel of Jesus Christ.* Translated by
John Bowden. Harrisburg, Penn.: Trinity Press, 2000.

Kelly, J. N. D. *Early Christian Doctrines.* New York: Harper & Row, 1958.

McDonald, Lee, and James A. Sanders, ed. *The Canon Debate.* Peabody, Mass.:
Hendrickson, 2002.

Pelikan, Jaroslav. *The Christian Tradition.* Chicago: University of Chicago Press,
1971.

Wright, N. T. *The Resurrection of the Son of God.* Minneapolis: Fortress, 2003.

Subject Index